Stress Free Finances

Leverage my 25+ years in finance to create

By
Jonathan Mills Patrick

Copyright © 2024 by Jonathan Mills Patrick.

All rights reserved. No part of this publication may be reproduced, distributed, or transmitted in any form or by any means, including photocopying, recording, or other electronic or mechanical methods, without the prior written permission of the publisher, except in the case of brief quotations embodied in critical reviews and certain other noncommercial uses permitted by copyright law.

Table of Contents

Introduction 1
Disclaimer 5
How to get the most out of this book 8
What this book isn't about 12
To win you have to think about 💵 differently 15
    A story about grit 16
Playing offense, i.e. makes more money 26
The Budget & Retirement Planning spreadsheet 30
    The B-word 32
    Budget Forecasting 38
    Personal Financial Statement 40
    Your, oh 💩 fund 42
    Life Insurance 44
    Investable Dollars 48
    Retirement Income Planning 49
    Section Wrap-up 51
Debt 52
    Common Debt Terms 54
    How Debt Gets Approved 56
    The Basics of Credit Reporting 58
    Credit Cards 63

- Vehicle loans ... 66
- Mortgage loans ... 73
- Student loans ... 78
- Debt snowballing ... 82
- Section Wrap-up ... 83
- Investments ... 85
  - Investment Fundamentals ... 86
  - Other Considerations ... 99
  - Investment Options ... 108
- Wrapping up ... 121
- Resources ... 123

Introduction

I can remember scrounging through my car's coin tray for enough money to buy something to eat. That happened more than once. Although, I don't remember them all, the time that springs to mind is when I was living off of Western Avenue, and I had driven to the local Long John Silvers. I remember sitting in the parking lot, counting up quarters, dimes, and nickels to see if I had enough. Long John's used to give people extra "crunchies" for free. Crunchies are the extra fried batter that is created when frying up people's orders. Long John's didn't charge for Crunchies. You just had to ask for them. So, I did. Every single time to make sure I was full.

The other core memory, I have of struggling financially comes from my early married life. To this day, my wife and I talk about whenever we couldn't justify buying new socks. It was that touch and go. When my wife, and I were first dating she was still in graduate school and I had just returned from Japan and was re-starting my professional career. She was living off of student loans and I was making a whopping $23,000 a year, and even that was what is called a draw, or essentially an advance against future earnings.

I'm not going to pretend that I grew up poor. I didn't. In fact, I grew up in an upper-middle class family. Still, we had our fair share of financial ups and downs, especially when my father decided to leave his impressive corporate career to start his own business. That period carries with it another memory centered around money.

I was the type of kid in high school who was more than happy to be by myself. One of my favorite activities was to go to the movies by myself. I can distinctly remember my father giving me cash to go to the movies, but I knew that he was burning through his life savings to get his business off the ground.

So, I do know what it's like to struggle financially. I've lived through the decisions about whether to buy food or buy an essential such as socks. Those decisions don't feel good. Sure, food is a basic need. But, not being able to buy socks? Really?

It will come as no shock to you that money is the number one stressor in life. According to some reports, 73% of Americans (where I live) rank finances as the number one stress point in life.

What if it didn't have to be that way? What if there was a way to live with stress-free finance? What would it be like to once and for all conquer the almighty dollar and instead of you serving money, you made your money serve you?

This is the part where I whip out my crystal ball. It tells me that you are thinking something along the lines of one of these scenarios: 1) I'm barely surviving, Jonathan. There is no way I can get ahead; 2) I've tried to take control of my money more times than I can count. This time won't be different; 3) Don't you dare say the B-word, i.e. budget, I hate those things; 4) I've read books like yours before, JP (you can call me that, it's cool), and there isn't anything new to learn.

Let's just agree right now that we are going to cut through the crap and be utterly transparent with one another.

1) So, you are barely surviving, eh? I hear you. I've been there. I got ahead. Was it easy? Hell no. Can you do it? Yep. If you want it bad enough. If not, go back to scrolling through social media. How is that working for you?

2) You don't think this time will be different? Let me challenge you with - do you always give up this easily on something that can be life-changing?

3) The B-word? Budgets suck. I'm going to give you tools that make it not suck. We won't be creating your average budgets. Or, should I say, we won't be just creating your average budget.

4) I see you. You're that person that has read all the books and watched all the videos. So, there is nothing new to learn? You might be right. But, perhaps, just maybe, the difference is that I'm going to give you frameworks that you can actually put into practice. I'm a life-long learner. You know what beats learning? Doing. You are a doer, right? Or, do you just talk a big game like everyone else?

I've been accused of jumping to the end-game too quickly. But, it has worked out pretty well for my family. So, I'm going to give away the punchline. Right now.

Stress Free Finances

I am not going to promise you that I can teach you to get rich. I'm only making you one promise. That alone is scary enough for me. But, we've got this, right?

If you get dead serious about taking control of your money you will eventually experience the peace that comes with stress-free finances.

But, wait, what does "eventually" mean? It means that I don't know how long this journey will take you. Some people will reach the stress-free state quicker than others. There are so many variables included that I can't tell you how long this will take. For example, I have an advantage that others normally don't have. I've built up 25+ years of finance experience and knowledge that I can leverage.

Wouldn't you love to be able to tap into that experience? Oh wait, you can. That is the entire reason I wrote this book. I'm sharing with you everything (ok everything I can think of) I've learned in over 25+ years in finance. From being involved in hundreds of millions of dollars in deals, to the tune of $800,000,000, to managing my own money. Is my family wealthy? Nope. But, what we are is stress-free. You can't put a price tag on that.

Disclaimer

The information contained in this book is for educational and informational purposes only and should not be construed as financial advice. Investing involves inherent risks, and past performance is not necessarily indicative of future results.

This book is not a substitute for professional financial or investment advice. The author recommends that you consult with a qualified financial professional before making any financial or investment decisions.

The author and publisher are not liable for any financial or investment decisions, losses, or damages resulting from the use of this information.

Jonathan Mills Patrick is a licensed life and health insurance agent, not an investment advisor. He is not providing or promoting personalized or individualized investment advice or information that is tailored to the needs of any particular recipient and does not guarantee the accuracy or completeness of the information provided in this book. All statements and expressions herein are the sole opinion of the author.

THE INFORMATION CONTAINED IN THIS BOOK IS NOT AND SHOULD NOT BE CONSTRUED AS FINANCIAL OR INVESTMENT ADVICE, AND DOES NOT PURPORT TO BE AND DOES NOT EXPRESS ANY OPINION AS TO THE PERFORMANCE OR PRICE AT WHICH THE SECURITIES OF ANY COMPANY MAY TRADE AT ANY

TIME. THE INFORMATION AND OPINIONS PROVIDED HEREIN SHOULD NOT BE TAKEN AS SPECIFIC ADVICE ON THE MERITS OF ANY FINANCIAL OR INVESTMENT DECISION. INVESTORS SHOULD MAKE THEIR OWN INVESTIGATION AND DECISIONS REGARDING THE PROSPECTS OF ANY COMPANY DISCUSSED HEREIN BASED ON SUCH INVESTORS' OWN REVIEW OF PUBLICLY AVAILABLE INFORMATION AND SHOULD NOT RELY ON THE INFORMATION CONTAINED HEREIN. INVESTORS SHOULD OBTAIN INDIVIDUAL INVESTMENT ADVICE BASED ON THEIR OWN CIRCUMSTANCES BEFORE MAKING AN INVESTMENT DECISION

No statement or expression of opinion, or any other matter herein, directly or indirectly, is an offer or the solicitation of an offer to buy or sell the securities or financial instruments mentioned.

Any projections, market outlooks or estimates herein are forward looking statements and are inherently unreliable. They are based upon certain assumptions and should not be construed to be indicative of the actual events that will occur. Other events that were not taken into account may occur and may significantly affect the returns or performance of the securities discussed herein. The information provided herein is based on matters as they exist as of the date of preparation and not as of any future date, and the author undertakes no obligation to correct, update or revise the information in this document or to otherwise provide any additional material.

The author does not accept any liability whatsoever for any direct or consequential loss howsoever arising, directly or indirectly, from any use of the information contained herein.

By reading this book you are indicating your consent and agreement to this disclaimer and our terms of use. Unauthorized reproduction of this book or its contents by photocopy, facsimile or any other means is illegal and punishable by law.

How to get the most out of this book

I've read a lot of books that didn't do a damn thing for me. They were a regurgitation of what I had already read one-hundred times over in other books. I don't want this book to be that for you. But, I know it's hard to promise that it won't be. Because, there are a lot of really solid financial advice books in the market.

Getting the most out of this book is going to require you to do something that the vast majority of readers rarely do. What is that? You need to commit to actually implementing some of what you read.

Don't just flip the pages while you are trying to fall asleep. I don't like slobber anyways. Now, I can't promise you that this book will be entertaining. In fact, the way I am writing this book is for it to be more educational than anything. So, it could be a snoozer. That's fine by me, as long as you learn how to live a stress-free financial life.

You won't need to implement every single thing I talk about. Because I am going to cover a really wide range of financial topics there is no way to be sure that everything I write about applies to every single reader. Although I'm confident that most of the content in this book applies to everyone, the reality is that there will always be edge cases. For example, you might already have an emergency fund set aside. If that is true, great. What you need to know is that isn't the case for a huge percentage of the population. So, I felt it was important to talk about in this book.

So, don't be bashful about skipping sections. Seriously. If you are really good at budgeting then there is no reason to download the template that is included, right? I mean, you already know how to budget, you have your own template that is helping you stay on track, and you are sticking to your budget. Right?

To help you implement what you read, I am going to go out of my way to give you actionable ways to make that happen. For example, when I talk about determining how much life insurance you should have, I'll be providing you with a template, in the form of a downloadable, to use in determining that number. While I'd like to think that my advice is valuable, **the real value in this book is going to be all the templates and resources that I created and found for you.** So, make sure you watch for the links to those digital assets. You can also find them in the Resources appendix.

Now, just in case you are a speed reader, howdoesthatworkanyways?Isn'titamazingthatthehumanbraincan worksoquicklytoturntextintosoundsinyourheadthatyoucanthenstor einshorttermmemorytobeaccessedatwhimwhenyouneedthatinform ation.

Sorry, I was messing with you. Are you still with me? Or, did you already zone out or start doom-scrolling through Instagram?

What I was saying was, in case you are the type that goes into auto-read mode, I'm going to be highlighting key phrases that you need to note. You should have figured out how I will do that by now, which is by using **bold text**. **Plus, for sections that are longer or full of information I'll provide you with a summary of key points. Finally, some sections use boxes such as below to call out important links. If you are not reading this digitally, those same links are at the end of the book in a Resources section, where the links are spelled out.**

File	Description	Status
Example	Example	Example

I know early I said that you can skip sections. That aside, I have tried to organize the book in two ways. First, I have started with the more simple financial concepts that are easier to consume. My thought is to use those concepts as building blocks as we build up towards the more advanced topics. Second, when possible, I structured sections in the order of areas that I would recommend attacking. For example, I agree with Dave Ramsey that you need to have a very basic emergency fund setup before you start paying down debt. So, the chapters are structured in that order to promote a step-by-step attack plan.

We will start with building up your knowledge around the key components of stress-free finances and then move on to more advanced topics.

Stress Free Finances

One more note before we move on. If a section is confusing, you have a question, or you just want to tell me that I'm wrong about something, simply send me an email at jonathan@jonathanmillspatrick.com. I'll do my best to answer your answers or attack your reputation for being a mean internet troll 😜.

What this book isn't about

If you came here looking for a get rich quick guide, go ahead and grab something to toss across the room. **Because you are going to be severely disappointed and frustrated.** By the way, I let my temper get the best of me once and I tossed a water bottle across the room which led to a super cool dent in my 12-string guitar. So, maybe on second thought, don't grab something to toss.

I'm taking an educational stance with the information I share. While there are some tactical tips included, I am mostly trying to improve your financial literacy.

The path to stress-free finances is littered with people, and gurus, darn those gurus, who promised people that getting control of your money was going to be easy. It's not. Using a phrase I used twice today already, it is going to get harder before it gets easier.

So, no get rich quick schemes ☑.

This book is also not for people who are looking for tips on how to be day traders in the stock market or real estate investors. While I have the experience to talk about those things, I've had personal success with both, I'm not going to do in depth in those topics. Those topics are so deep that they could be books in and of themselves. Heck, they just might be one day soon. Hint, hint.

Stress Free Finances

Alright, so no day trading or real estate investing techniques ☑. No angel investing tips either. Which I also have a ton of experience with.

This book is not going to cover advanced financial topics. For one simple reason. You don't need advanced financial knowledge to achieve stress-free finances. We are going to leverage Pareto's Principle, otherwise known as the 80/20 rule, and focus on the 20% of the knowledge that will lead to the 80% results. That is what the typical person needs.

There is one more thing this book isn't about. Really long-winded. I don't have any preconceived notions about how long this book should and shouldn't be. Each section isn't going to be long enough to get my point across and to give you the information you need to improve your financial life. Nothing more, nothing less. So, if that means a section is only one paragraph long, then so be it. As long as I can get across what I think you need to know about that topic in so few words then we will call that section complete and move on.

Now, will this book be long? Relatively speaking. But, not because I decided to be verbose or because my book deal said that the book has to be 50,000 words long. It will be long because there are a lot of topics I want to cover and I want you to get your money's worth.

Don't get overwhelmed. The key is to attack areas of your financial life in steps or phases. You don't need to feel the pressure to do everything I talk about in the next month or even year.

What you do need to do is get started. Build some momentum in your financial life. Get some early wins. Which is why we are going to start with something that most finance books ignore. How to make more money.

But, before we get to that, I need you to shift your mindset about money.

Stress Free Finances

To win you have to think about 📖 differently

There is something about finances that is tough for a lot of people. Most people have been taught not to talk about money. It is treated like some taboo subject that shouldn't be mentioned. If you are a Harry Potter fan, it's like saying his name. You know, Volker...just kidding, chill out.

One of the reasons that so many people struggle with finances is because money is treated like voodoo. I believe that being open about it can make a huge difference. Simply talking about money allows people who aren't as versed in financial matters to learn from others. So, stop treating money as some mystical thing.

The other issue is that people simply aren't disciplined enough. They allow their emotions to drive them to make terrible financial decisions. If you are completely honest with yourself, **your inability to control your emotions and the need to have your ego stroked is consistently derailing you from taking control of your financial future**.

There is no better example than the car industry. Consumers will go into massive amounts of debt at high interest rates on a luxury car simply because it makes them feel special. I know of people whose car payments are almost as much as their rent or house payment. All for a depreciating asset now less. I'm not making fun of anyone. I've done it more times than I can count. At one point our house payment was less than $1,000 and our car payments were more than $1,000 per month. Few people really need an SUV that can carry fourteen people and groceries at the same time.

Having stress-free finances is all about discipline and perseverance, collectively known as grit. If there is one thing I have a lot of it's grit. Below, as an added bonus, I've captured a story about grit, I hope you enjoy it.

A story about grit

We were on the fourth and last Saturday of testing. I had been told that the test was more of a formality. That I had already done more than enough to pass. But it didn't feel like that was the case. It felt like the instructor was bound and determined to make me want to quit.

Each prior Saturday's worth of testing had become increasingly difficult. The first Saturday had begun with a simple one-mile run. I would become much more of a runner in the years to come. But, at the time, my fitness level was built more around maximum-level burst and recovery-style cardio. Not the sustained periods of moderate output that come with long runs. Still, I had prepared some for the exam and was the first to finish the one-mile jog.

Because of my personality and the fact that I was the head instructor, I took a moment to survey how the other candidates were doing. They hadn't prepared as much as I had, but, on average, they were doing fine. That is, except for Jeffrey.

Jeffrey was a highly intelligent pre-teen. He was also overweight and had terrible personal hygiene. His hygiene was bad enough that most times when he showed up for a class, I would have to sneak and Lysol his sneakers because they would make the whole studio smell awful. Multiple attempts to persuade Jeffrey to wear socks had failed.

As I watched Jeffrey complete only the first four laps of the run, I knew he wouldn't make it without intervention. The tears rolling down his cheeks told me that he knew it as well. I knew that there was still a lot of activity about to be thrown at us once the run was finished, and we were back at the studio. Going back out for what would amount to nearly an extra mile of running wasn't appealing. But, I couldn't let Jeffrey fail. So, I ran back out onto the course and fell in pace with Jeffrey.

I don't remember exactly what I said to him that day. All I can remember is being extremely frustrated that he was crying during a black belt exam. I suspect, I muttered to him the creed we had both been taught by the owner of the studio, who was my instructor. That creed was:

"As a dedicated student of the martial arts, I will live by the principles of the black belt. Modesty, courtesy, integrity, self-control, <u>perseverance</u>, and indomitable spirit."

While I've tried to live by all of those principles, it is the last two principles, perseverance, and indomitable spirit that seem to have shaped who I am more than the others, i.e. grit. I would later teach those same principles to my own students in the form of a mantra - He who gets tired first loses.

Those who have trained with me and under me will know that mantra all too well. The black belt tests that I have administered to my own students are proof that like my own black belt exams (because I have my 2nd-degree black belt, I took the exams twice), the exam has very little to do with skill. By the time you get to a black belt exam, at least the way my instructor and I designed it, you have already proven you have the skill. The exam is more about pushing you well beyond your comfort level and whether or not you will quit. It's about testing if you will give up so close to a significant accomplishment.

A one-mile run doesn't sound so bad. But, for people who aren't fans of running, it feels like torture. Except that the real torture is knowing that the run is merely the beginning of the day's activities.

By the time I coaxed Jeffrey into finishing the run, we were both running low on time. You see, the sooner you finish the run, the more time you have to rest, stretch back out, and get some water before the next activity begins. Having gone back out onto the track with Jeffrey, I had foregone nearly all the spare time I would have by finishing my own mile quickly.

Following the run, the next round of exercises is a few hours' worth of punch-kick combinations, both into the air and into pads of all sorts. Not only is it taxing, but it also becomes very monotonous. The repetition is meant to wear you further down. But, it has another effect. Because the exercises become so monotonous and you are so tired, it is human nature to go on autopilot. After all, the candidate has done these combinations more times than they can count by the time; they are testing for a black belt. And that is where the danger lies.

Eventually, your mind will wander. This is likely a self-defense mechanism, helpful in allowing you to forget just how tired you really are. The problem is that the instructor leading the exam will notice when you start to zone out. When that happens, the distracted student and the rest of the testing group are punished with extra exercises or in some cases, another one-mile run. I wouldn't begin to compare the difficulty level to something like basic training in the military. However, the process of breaking down the participants is similar.

Jeffrey got distracted and went on autopilot more times than I can remember. This meant that day one of the exams was easily an hour or two longer than it should have been if all of the students had performed even moderately well. Once we were dismissed that day, I walked Jeffrey out to his mother's car. After giving his mother the details of the day, I encouraged Jeffrey to make a very hard decision. I suggested ,to him to go home and rest. Then the next day, and every day until our second Saturday's worth of testing, I told him to look in the mirror and ask himself if he had the grit to go through all that we had just experienced at least three more times. I recommended he save himself and the rest of the students from three more days of hell if he didn't.

You might find it strange that someone's instructor recommends that they consider quitting. I can honestly reflect on that moment and tell you that my speech to Jeffrey was part truth and part reverse psychology. If he didn't have the grit to gut it out, I didn't think he deserved a black belt. Obtaining a black belt in most commercialized martial arts these days is not the same as it used to be. When martial arts had just started to gain popularity, someone with a black belt was a true expert at their craft. You knew that they had earned it. Sure, some black belts were more skilled than others. But, if someone had a black belt, you knew that they were the best version of themselves when they received it. Nowadays, I'm not so sure that is the case.

Jeffrey was not the best version of himself at the time. When the next Saturday rolled around, he had chosen to drop out of the exam. Fortunately, many months later, he would return and complete the exam. As the studio's head instructor, I felt like a failure. That manifested itself in throwing myself all-in into the rest of my 1st-degree black belt exam. I can't pretend my mind and body didn't try to go on autopilot over the next three Saturdays. But if they did, it was rare. Between wanting to be an example to the other students and realizing that I was about to accomplish one of my lifetime dreams of earning a black belt, I attacked the exam as if my life depended on it.

Stress Free Finances

The fourth Saturday is reserved strictly for sparring. Every single student, past and present, black belts and lower belts are invited to come spar with the candidates. Once again, the day is designed to make you want to quit. Imagine being exhausted and having to fight someone who is completely fresh. When that happens, it is easy to let a strike slip out a little too hard. If you hit someone too hard, you are given extra push-ups to do. If you don't fight hard enough, you are told to put your shoes on and "take a hike," otherwise known as logging another mile. Finding a happy medium between not fighting too hard and not fighting hard enough is impossible. Another intentional design of the black belt exam. And, if you take notice, a theme in life. Finding balance is insanely difficult to do.

As the day of sparring nears its end, if they are not zoned out and paying attention, a student will notice that a particular black belt is coming back to fight them more quickly than the line should have allowed. In my case, it was Peyman. He was one of my toughest opponents in sparring. Most of the time, I would win our matches. At least, that is how I remember our sparring sessions. I was a little faster and taller, so I had length as my advantage. Plus, I was younger. I could hit him first more times than not. But, Peyman hit hard. So, even if you hit him first, he would make you pay.

I had just fought Peyman one or two opponents prior. Yet, there he was standing next in line to fight me again. I knew we had to be close to the end of the exam. The bell rang, and he charged straight into me. By this time, I was beyond tired, and he could tell. Willing to take my preemptive shots, Peyman simply absorbed my attacks and started landing heavy shots of his own. This was all on purpose, of course. He was forcing me to make one final push. As the adrenaline shot through me, I landed a hook kick that tore the headgear off his head. Grabbing the headgear off the floor, I roared a challenge at Peyman and then flung my headgear across the room. My instructor called time while Peyman and I smiled and then hugged. The exam was over.

Kneeling before my head instructor at the belt ceremony, I was told to take my brown belt, otherwise known as "scum belt," off. Just as I thought the exam was over, my instructor, with my black belt in hand, smiled and gave me one last assignment - 100 pushups. Most people can't do 100 straight push-ups, let alone after hours of sparring. I remember flying through them without a pause or change in my form. That moment was all about grit.

In 1996 I became the Grand Champion of the Tennessee Karate Circuit by finishing first in Kumite (fighting) in my weight division, first in forms, and second in weapons forms. Later on, in my martial arts career, I would transition over into competing in mixed martial arts (MMA) fights and even go on to fight some overseas in Japan. I did not lose a fight in my natural weight class.

What leads to that level of success? I wasn't the biggest or strongest competitor. I was 6'3" and all of 175 pounds, dripping wet. I was tall and lean. Probably too lean.

Stress Free Finances

When I started competing in MMA, it was so early that the first Ultimate Fighting Championship (UFC) hadn't even happened, and most fighters were either one of two types of fighters - punch/kick fighters or grapplers. Very few fighters had deep experience as a stand-up artist and knew how to grapple. I was the exception. Although I had started my martial arts career learning all kinds of punch/kick styles, my instructor knew that grappling was important. So much so that we were the first studio in Tennessee to learn Brazilian jiu-jitsu (BJJ) under the esteemed Gracie family, so, some of the credit goes to timing. Another portion of the credit goes to how strategic I was as a fighter. My mentors all called me a very "cerebral" fighter. They also said I was a "gifted fighter."

However, the real credit goes to the mental edge I held over most fighters. I simply outworked just about everyone I trained with, sparred with, or fought against because I had a level of grit to see my goals come to fruition that few can sustain.

I can't pretend my mentality was always that way before my martial arts training began, or that I have been able to carry forward with the same level of perseverance and determination as I have gotten older. In fact, my martial arts career almost didn't happen.

I was 15 years old when I asked my father to let me take karate lessons. I had been experimenting with, and subsequently quitting, all kinds of hobbies. One month it was archery. The next month I was "into" music. On and on it went. Doubting that I would stick with it, plus using a bit of his own reverse psychology, my father told me that I'd never get my black belt. Flash forward to my second-degree black belt ceremony, where I hugged my father and whispered to him, "You were right. I got my second-degree black belt". Looking back now, I can tell you without any doubt that who I am today is because of my martial arts training. It taught me many important lessons I have leveraged in business and life.

Now, 33 years into my martial arts life, I have to admit that some of those lessons have ebbed in and out of my life. Admittedly, I've lost some of my mental edge. Life has a way of beating people down. I have no exception. The world has just gone through two years of a global COVID-19 pandemic, where how we have lived has been, forever, changed. Coupled with losing my father and my only sibling, my older brother, my mental state has been pushed to its limits. So much that a nasty habit has been creeping into my life. Lately, when things get tough, I just walk away. I've allowed myself to quit on my dreams.

Fortunately, in the past few months, I've started to come back to the idea that the mental edge I used to have wasn't just useful as a martial artist. It has shaped virtually every other aspect of my life. As I regained my confidence, I remembered the power that perseverance and determination can play in a person's life and the role a positive mindset can play in helping you accomplish your goals. And it all started with remembering one of my mantras.

"He Who Gets Tired First Loses"

Stress Free Finances

Playing offense, i.e. makes more money

Most finance books talk about budgeting and saving money. They focus on defensive tactics for getting ahead. While that is important, as I stated earlier, it's hard to save your way to abundant wealth.

Instead, let's talk about offense first, rather than defense.

Would you like to play a game? I love games. What does the following graph represent?

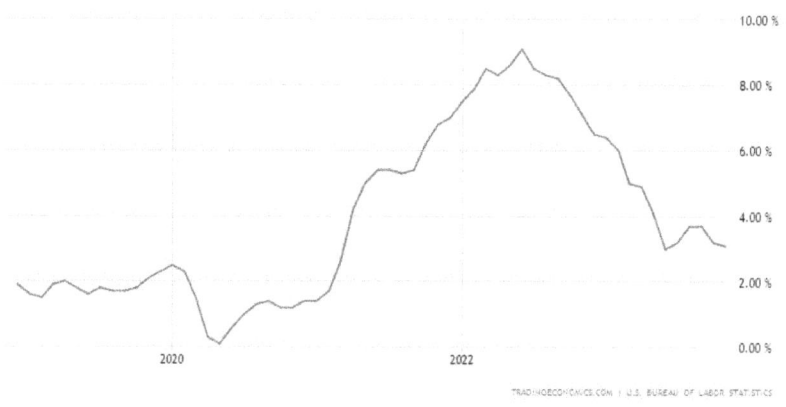

That, my friends, is the rate of inflation in the United States from 2019-2023 (roughly). The top end was 9% inflation. In case you don't know, a typical targeted rate of inflation is 2-3%. So, for over 1.5 years the U.S. had a rate of inflation that was between 2x-3x that targeted range. Does that sound like a good thing? It isn't. But, that's what happens when you pump trillions of dollars into the economy in the form of stimulus checks.

Let's cut to my point, in the spirit of avoiding a political debate.

Stress Free Finances

When inflation is running at 5-10%, month-over-month, the average person can't save their way to a balanced budget. Unless you are literally living paycheck to paycheck, it doesn't matter how disciplined you are at creating and sticking to a budget, avoiding $5 coffee at Starbucks isn't going to make that big of a difference. Think about it this way. Every month that $5 sits in the bank, you are losing value at the rate of inflation. So, at a 10% inflation rate, that $5 is now worth $4.50, then almost $4, and so on. Conversely, trying to earn 10% interest on that $5 you saved is not easy.

That is why I believe that one of the best ways to create stress-free finances is to focus on increasing your income.

There are a lot of ways to make more money. You could:
- Ask for a raise at work.
- Find a new job that pays you more money.
- Take on a second job.
- Start a freelance business.

Before you get too excited, if the last option sounds sexy, I want to be real transparent that starting a business is hard. I have spent countless hours at night (I'm typing this at 8:12pm) grinding away various business ventures. Most of my friends, and even my older brother, have admitted that they could never dedicate as much energy and time as I have to building an extra income. I get it. There are plenty of nights that I would much rather be gaming or watching a show than working.

Stress Free Finances

Why would I say in one sentence that you should consider figuring out how to make more money, and in the next try to scare you with how much work is involved? Because lying to you doesn't do either of us any good. But, if making more money sounds interesting, keep reading. Otherwise, skip to the next section. Still with me? Great.

Over the past ten or more years I have been freelancing on the side. Although took some time to get traction, today my side businesses generate on average between $30,000-$50,000 per year in additional income for my family. We have used that money to build up our emergency fund to over six-figures, pay off all of our debt, minus our mortgage, and invest in various investments.

My first venture was doing the bookkeeping for a local business. Paul was one of my banking customers and after getting to know him it was clear that his bookkeeper, his ex-mother-in-law, was terrible at keeping up with their financial statements. Paul had no way of telling how much money was coming and where they were spending all of their money. At the time I was looking for an extra source of income, so I offered to manage his books for him. I charged Paul $450 per month. Originally this work took me about 10 hours per week. Although my equivalent hourly rate was terrible, I got paid in another form of currency as well. Education. I was learning how to run my own business. Over time, I was able to cut the time down to about 10 hours per month, which was a much more reasonable hourly rate. I still use the lessons I learned from that first opportunity today.

Since then I have experimented with lots of other business models. Some have worked and others have not. Still, I consider all of those experiences valuable, because I learned a lot of lessons that continue to help me in business today. Those same lessons are available to you, for free.

Earlier I promised you that the value of this book would be in all of the templates that I will be providing you. **Here is your first template. It's free.**

Type	Description	Link to content
Email course	7-day email course that will teach you my formula for starting a freelance business.	Head here.

If you decide that earning some extra cash is a good idea, that course will walk you through the process I used when creating my own freelance business. Your goal should be to generate the equivalent of one-month's worth of your normal income. If you can do that, you just gave yourself a 8% raise. Pretty cool, huh? Plus, you are generating money that can be put to use in other ways.

Stress Free Finances

The Budget & Retirement Planning spreadsheet

To help you work through the <u>next few sections</u>, I've built you a spreadsheet template that will take your inputs and create various financial planning outputs. Each section builds upon the data entered in the previous sections.

You will want to download the template and have it at the ready as you read the next sections. You should also watch the videos inside the course. They go into further explanation about how to use the template. One note on the template, I wanted to make it completely free, but the site that I use to host my products (Gum road) won't allow a product that takes up a large amount of storage to be completely free. Plus, some unscrupulous people have been downloading my free content and then using it to sell to make money for themselves. So, I've marked it as cheap as I can - $1. However, **you can get it for FREE if you use the code SFFBOOK at checkout**. You can get the template at the link below.

What you will get is a set of training videos that guide you through how to complete the spreadsheet and a downloadable Excel template. The template will help you plan out the below items, which I talk more about in the following sections.

- Build a budget.

Stress Free Finances

- A budget forecasting tool that will help you see the impact of various financial decisions.
- Calculate your personal net worth.
- Establish how much of an emergency fund you need to have.
- Calculate how much life insurance you should have in place.
- Establish how much discretionary income/money you have for use in investing.
- Calculate how much money you will need to retire.

Type	Description	Link to content
Video course and Excel template	A semi-automated budgeting and retirement planning spreadsheet and the associated training videos. **Use the code SFFBOOK at checkout to get it for free.**	Head here.

A few notes about the template:

1) I would start with two copies. One that you save somewhere and don't touch. Consider this a backup copy in case you mess up something, like a formula, and you

can't figure out how to fix it. If you haven't gone too far down that road, the undo button in Excel is your friend.

2) Be sure you read the Instructions tab first. In case you are being lazy, shame on you, the key is that you can enter data in the gray cells. Don't touch anything that is a normal white cell, because it is likely to be using a formula.

The B-word

Look, I get it. No one enjoys budgeting. It isn't fun to have to tell yourself or your kids that you can't afford something because it isn't in your budget at the moment. You know what else isn't fun? Being broke because you are undisciplined.

You have to be disciplined with where you spend your money and you have to do that for an extended period of time to get ahead. Jumping on a budgeting bandwagon and then falling off the wagon a month later doesn't do you any good. That said, neither does being so restrictive with your budget that you can't enjoy life. Finance gurus love picking on people who spend $5 for coffee. Others promote a beans and rice diet, because it's cheap, until you are in a better financial position.

Here's the problem with those types of budgets - they aren't sustainable for the majority of people and they leave you miserable. Now listen, I get why that type of advice is given. Because, for the undisciplined, allowing any straying from a budget means they will go completely off the rails. But, I've seen it time and again where people lock down their budgets so tightly that they don't get to enjoy their life. The reality is that life can be very short. So, you have to find ways to enjoy it. If that means that you treat yourself to a fancy coffee every once in a while then so be it.

There are a few ways to go about creating a budget. Before I share my favorite method, let's set some ground rules.

1) You must be conservative. I want you to underestimate your income and overestimate your expenses.
2) For your income use <u>annual averages</u>, not your best or worst months. Also, use post-tax, post-benefit numbers. If you have salaried jobs then that should be pretty easy. Just use the number that hits your bank account each pay period. Do not, under any circumstances, include bonuses or irregular income months, unless you can demonstrate a historical pattern for that income. For example, if you are a realtor and your best month was $10k per month, do not set your annual income at $120k. Sorry realtors, I used to see this example all the time when approving auto and home loans. Instead, take an average of your last few years of income.
3) The same is true for expenses. Use annual averages. This works best because some expenses vary in amount, meaning they are variable not fixed. Variable expenses include utilities, groceries, etc.

4) Budgets should be living documents. Meaning, don't just build yours and then leave it collecting dust. How you track your performance against your budget is up to you. There are a few options for this:
   a) If you know how to use Excel, you could alter my template. For example:
      i) Right click on the Budget tab and choose Duplicate. Now right click on Column C and insert a row to the right. In Row 3, name it something like Actual spend.
   b) You could pay for one of the more automated solutions. Here I would normally recommend Mint, but that is being shut down. Other options that exist at this time include True bill/Rocket Money.

Where I would **focus most of your energy inside your budget is on the variable expenses**. It's likely that your fixed expenses are already set. I like you to focus on variable expenses because a few of those categories are where I see people slip up the most. The best example is eating out. Yes, there are instances where you can eat out cheaper than you can make a certain meal at home. But, that isn't always true, and generally speaking, if you shop well, you can feed yourselves for less by eating at home. Case in point, just yesterday we ordered out from a local restaurant. My daughter had a pasta dish and I had a wedge salad. It was $32, without tax and tip!

That said, **fixed expenses are where you need to pay extra attention to their cost <u>at the time of purchase</u>**. Many fixed expenses are financed, like cars, and making a mistake when you purchase them, like agreeing to too high a price or a high interest rate, will cost you a lot of money until that debt is gone.

The Pay Yourself First budget method

One of the methods around budgeting is the 50/30/20 rule. Where 50% of your money goes toward needs, 30% toward wants, and 20% toward savings. That concept leads me to my favorite budgeting method. It is called the "Pay Yourself First" method.

With most budgets people focus on allocating their money to other people first. Their home lender or daycare. Try flipping that mentality around. Pay yourself before you allocate money for anyone else. The way to do that is to make your first budget item the amount of money you want to save each month. Let's say you make $3k per month and your goal is to save 5% of your income, or $150 per month. That $150 should be the first number you enter into your budgeting spreadsheet. I even have a line item for that in my template called "Deposit into savings". It should be in the Investments section. If you really want to make sure that you pay yourself first, have that $150 come straight out of your paycheck and be directly deposited into your savings account. That way it never hits your checking account. That is exactly what I do. If things are so tight that you don't have any money to set aside to pay yourself then let's make that a goal. Maybe by eliminating some unnecessary spending or figuring out how to make some extra money. Later we are going to look at what to do with the money you are paying yourself.

Now that you have paid yourself first, you can start allocating dollars to other expenses. I would start with the expenses that are non-negotiable. The last categories you should be allocating budget to are things that are 1) a want not a need; 2) variable. **The rough order you should follow under this budget method should look like:**

1) Pay yourself first.
2) Food, shelter, and clothing - this should be basic, no frill minimums. You can come back later and bump those budgets up if you have enough left over. Also, don't forget associated expenses. For example, for shelter, you will have utilities and insurance (even if you rent, I recommend renter's insurance because it is so affordable).
3) Transportation - depending on if public transportation is viable. I would factor in some money for a vehicle and its associated expenses like gas and insurance. Again, no frills. We all love fancy cars. However, the truth is that a low cost sedan will get you around town just as much as a huge SUV. Again, you can buff up this budget when you have money left over.
4) Insurance (health) - next I'd put money aside for health insurance. If you have it from your work and it's auto-deducted from your paycheck then you can skip this item.

One note here. I've talked to people who think health insurance isn't a must. It is in my opinion. Especially if you have kids.

5) Cellphone - cellphones are expensive. Still, I see them as an important budget item. Now, I'm not saying you need the top end iPhone. Those things currently cost $1,600.

6) Debts - I consider items 1-5 to be necessary, for most people. Once you have those bases covered (as skinny as you can) you should be budgeting to pay back any debts you have. That would include credit cards, student loans, etc.

After 1-6 are handled you can think about things like entertainment or setting aside a budget for gifts to family and friends.

Is this budget perfect? No, it is not. Every budget is only as good as the person creating it. It requires you to be realistic. For example, one issue with the Pay Yourself First method is that you are opting to save money before you pay down your debt, I.e. Dave Ramsey's Debt Snowball approach. But, saving all that money won't do you any good if you are dipping into savings to cover overspending. Regardless, my personal belief is that paying yourself first creates a habit of spending that is important. Besides, the money is there to pay off debts, or any other activity, should you choose to go that route.

Regardless of the method you choose for setting up your budget, go ahead and stop reading and get your budget setup. This is critical, because it will feed into the next few sections.

Budget Forecasting

For this section we will **be on the Budget Forecasting tab** in the template. Remember, only change things in the gray cells, don't touch anything in white!

Where you spend your money will change over time. A common example of this is spending more money as your income increases. Such as buying a new car because you got a promotion. You have to look sharp after all, right?

What I'd rather you do is learn to "lock-in" your spending. In a perfect world, I'd tell you to save or invest every extra dollar you make, above the minimal amount to satisfy your budget. But, it's probably unrealistic to ask you to keep your level of spending the same for the rest of your life.

When you created your budget, you probably built it based on where things stand today, or in a slightly more disciplined state. Now I want you to create multiple budget scenarios.

- Column C, Scenario #1 - Create a "skinny budget."
    - This will be the tightest budget you can stick to. It's for when things are really, really tough. Be ruthless here. Imagine you just got laid off and you absolutely have to cut expenses. The idea is to get down to a baseline budget that you could live on if

you had to. The other great thing about establishing a skinny budget is that it shows you how you could live on less if you needed.

- Column D, Scenario #2 - Increasing income.
  - Let's pretend that you got a promotion or raise that you were hoping for. Maybe you found a new job paying you more money. Or, maybe you start a side hustle that will create some income. Use this column to see the impact of that additional income. I recommend copying over all of the expenses from Column B, using copy/paste, and then simply entering new income amounts.
- Column E, Scenario #3 - New expense/Increasing expense..
  - I once heard a statistic that said 43% of people that buy a new home also buy a new car within six months. Let's use this scenario for that dream car or home you have been thinking about. Copy over your income and expenses from Column B and then play with changes. I used this approach when we were looking at buying a new home. I left our budget flat except for home expenses such as the mortgage payment, insurance, utilities, trash, security system, etc. Or, it doesn't have to be such a huge expense. You could play with the impact of eating out more in this column.

You don't have to use my above examples. You can use the Budget Forecast tab to play around with all kinds of scenarios. Another time I used it was to see the impact on our budget of when our daughter was getting her driver's license. Fortunately, we had been saving for some time for a car for her, but I still wanted to see what the other expenses, like gas and insurance, would do to our spending levels.

Personal Financial Statement

If you really want to win at the money game, you have to think about it completely differently. One aspect of that is to move away from only thinking about money in terms of income and expenses, i.e. a budget. **Your goal should be to think about money in terms of assets and liabilities**. Which is where a personal financial statement comes into play.

Assets are things you own that are worth money. Another way to think about some assets is that they have the ability to make you more money. **Liabilities are things that you owe to others**. It's possible for something to be both an asset and a liability. For example, if you have a house with a mortgage. The house might be worth $300,000 (asset) but you owe a lender $200,000 (liability). In that example you would have $100,000 in equity.

Head to the Personal Financial Statement tab in the template.

A PFS is meant to track your net worth. When someone is a millionaire they don't have one million dollars in annual income, although they could. What they are saying is that they have one million dollars in net worth. Their assets are worth one million dollars more than the liabilities they owe.

Starting at the top of each category, assets are listed in order of liquidity. Liquidity signals how quickly an asset can be converted into cash. That is why cash in bank accounts is listed first. It's already liquid. Whereas, it would take you some time to sell your house and convert your equity into cash. Liabilities are listed in order of the timeframe that they are done. Anything that is due within the next 12-months comes first.

To complete your PFS, I recommend you be as accurate as possible. With one caveat. If it takes you more than a few hours to gather all of the right information then you need to stop. We don't need accuracy down to the last penny. For example, if you aren't sure what your home is worth try looking at similar homes for sale on Zillow or Realtor. Just make sure you aren't letting bias creep into the valuation. Rough estimates are fine for this go around. The idea is to get an idea on where you stand. There are a few things I want you to watch for, once you have completed this exercise.

1) The first thing to look at is cell C29, the one in green or orange. That is your net worth. Green means that you have a positive net worth. Meaning you could liquidate every asset you have, pay off all of your liabilities, and have some money left over. If it's orange, you owe too much money.

2) If cell C29 is green, let's dig deeper to see what the root of that is. For many households it will be the equity in your home that is helping. If, on the other hand, you have a ton of cash on hand, let's look at putting some of that money to work. That will be more clear in the section on emergency funds.

3) If cell C29 is orange, by a significant amount, then you likely need to make some serious changes to the financial decisions you are making to take back control. Sometimes people experience life events that force them into a bad financial position, such as huge medical expenses. But, in most cases it's their own decisions. If you are seeing orange you need to refocus on a realistic budget, save more money, pay-off some debt (which could mean selling a car or house that is too expensive), or figure out how to make more money.

I've heard it said that the wealthy think in terms of their balance sheet. That is another term used for a PFS. You may not be there today, especially if you are living paycheck to paycheck. But, start training your brain to think that way regardless. It will be helpful when you have more money to work with.

Your, oh 💩 fund

The fun thing about self-publishing a book is that you get to use inappropriate emoji's.

Stress Free Finances

Anyway, in case you haven't heard this statistic before, it is really quoted that the average U.S. household can't afford a $400 emergency. While the exact amount the average person has in savings is disputed, the fact remains that consumer savings is down.

For example, the Consumer Financial Protection Board (CFPB) report, back in 2022, that 37% of households didn't have more than one-month's worth in an emergency fund. In fact, the amount consumers are saving per month has been coming down, except for when the government was handing out money during the COVID-19 period, since the 1970s.

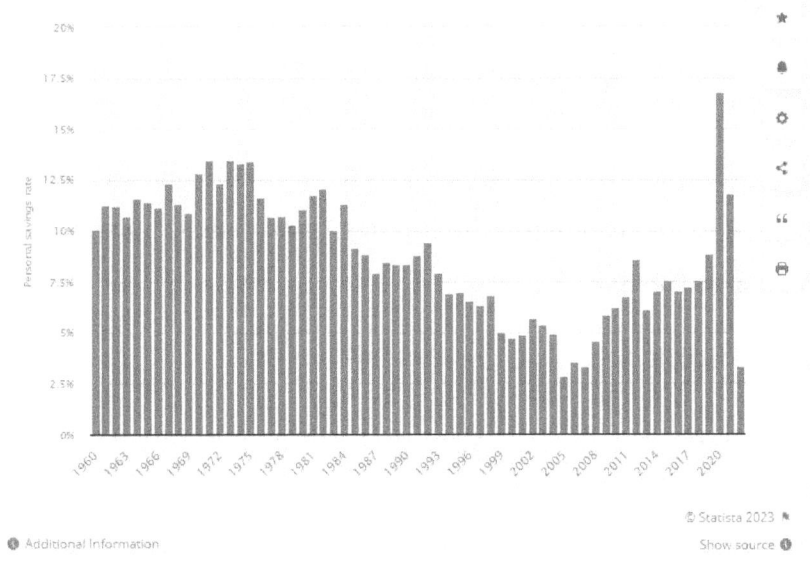

From a high of about 13% of household income being saved per year to the current value of only 3.31%, according to Statist. If you make the current average household income in the U.S., about $74,000, and you are saving the current average of 3.31%, that means you are only setting aside about $2,450 per year. Don't get me wrong, that's a start. But, you are still one large emergency expense, car repair or a plumbing issue at your house, away from your savings being wiped out.

That's why **the goal is to build up between 3-12 months worth of an emergency fund**. Why such a range? Because, the amount of money you want in an emergency fund will vary based on all kinds of factors. For example, if your company is known for doing layoffs and the economy is getting ugly you should consider having a larger fund. If you aren't sure what goal to set,

I'd shoot for 6 months worth on an emergency fund.

Alternatively, there is such a thing as having too much cash in the bank. That's why, later, we will visit the Investable Dollars tab in the template. For now, **if you have completed the prior tabs in the template the Emergency Fund Calculation should be done already**.

Life Insurance

I'm not here trying to sell you life insurance, although I am a licensed agent. But, I want you to have at least some life insurance in place. Why? Because it has worked well for my family, twice. Four years apart we lost my father and my only sibling, my brother. Losing a loved one is devastating. The good news is, for my mother and my sister-in-law, they both had license insurance policies in place. That left their loved ones with some financial assistance.

Conversely, I have heard one story after another where someone passed away prematurely and there was no life insurance in place. One husband lost a wife that was making over $200,000 per year. They were terrible at saving and without life insurance to replace that income stream the remaining family members had to sell their home, move into an apartment, and the husband had to take on extra jobs.

The method the template uses for calculating your life insurance needs is based on an industry formula called DIMEF. It calculates the amount of insurance you would need to have in place to:

- (D) pay off all your debts (otherwise the debtors could come after your loved ones for payment).
- (I) replace 10 years of income. This may sound like a lot, but trust me, it isn't. When my brother passed away he was just over 50. He had a lot of earning potential left that his family is missing out on.
- (M) pay off your mortgage. We did this for my mother when my father passed away.
- (E) cover future educational costs for dependents. This is the only field in the template where you need to add estimates. Everything else is pre-filled from the prior tabs.

- (F) cover funeral expenses. I have input the national average already. Honestly, many families spend more than the amount I used.

Understand that insurance policy premiums are based on a variety of factors that include your age, your health, etc. I always recommend working with an agent that is not tied to a particular company. That way they can provide you with quotes from multiple sources. The company you choose to buy your policy from needs to have 1) an affordable price; 2) a strong financial rating, so that they are unlikely to go out of business; 3) a history of paying life insurance claims. Some companies will try to make it almost impossible to file a claim.

You probably know that there are a variety of types of life insurance. I'm going to talk about the two most common forms I see.

Term life insurance

This is by far the most affordable and best policy to have in place for the vast majority of people. Term life insurance is a policy that pays a benefit to your beneficiaries if you die during a set period of time, i.e. a term. For example, if you take a term life insurance policy with a 30-year term at the age of 25, then the policy will pay the benefit if you pass away up until you are 55 years old. I have a 30-year term policy myself, that I took out when I was in my forties and it costs me under $200 per month for a large amount of money. It's not uncommon for term insurance policies to cost between $20-$50 per month.

Whole life insurance

Whole life insurance is in force your entire life. As long as you pay the premiums. The reason some people don't recommend whole life insurance is that it has higher premiums. Typically 2-3x that of term insurance. For example, the cost of my personal whole life policy premium is about the same as my term life policy but the face value is one-tenth that of my term life policy.

The premiums are higher because it also builds up a cash value. Some call that cash value an investment. I don't think of it that way. Because in many instances you could invest the difference in premium into another investment and get a better return. The cash value is more like a forced savings account that you can access if necessary. Also, the cash value in a whole life policy can be used to keep your policy in place if you run into a situation where you can't afford to make the premium payments for a period of time.

I do personally believe in whole life insurance, in the right instances. My father had a whole life policy in place when he passed away later in life.

One last note. A lot of people I speak to want to include life insurance benefits they get from a job in their DIMEF calculation. I don't consider that at all. I just consider it an extra benefit. Even though my brother's work-based life insurance policy paid out when we passed away. Why? Because the moment you change jobs, and most people will change multiple times, that policy is no longer in effect and you have lost any and all built up value. Policies that you put in place outside of your job are yours, forever. Unless you stop paying the premiums.

Investable Dollars

There is such a thing as having too much money in cash. Any amount of money beyond your emergency fund goal should be invested in some fashion. In today's environment, you can keep your cash liquid in a high-yield savings account that is earning 4% or more. But, that isn't always the case. In many instances, people have excess cash sitting in a low-yield checking account that is earning less than half a percent per year. Half a percent is better than nothing, right? Sure. But, you aren't really earning half a percent. You are losing money, because inflation is eating away at the value of your cash. The Federal government typically targets between 2-3% inflation. So, **as long as you aren't earning a yield that is higher than inflation you are losing money**. That's why, any amount of cash beyond your emergency fund goal should be put to work.

I would start with using excess cash to pay down debt. There are some money experts who will say that you should never pay debt where the interest rate is less than the rate you can earn on that same amount of money. Let me argue their case for a moment. For example, if you used $10k to pay off a car loan that had a 5% interest rate, or lower, which wasn't uncommon for strong credit profiles in the early 2020s, you could, possibly, have earned 8% in an S&P 500 fund. That's a 3% gain you are giving up by paying off the debt instead of investing that money. Still, my advice is to pay off all your debts, except your mortgage (because that is usually too large to pay off quickly). There is just a piece of mind that comes with no debt.

The Investable Dollars tab in the template assumes you have already paid off all of your debt, or that you didn't take my advice and you decided to invest your money instead. That's cool. It's your money, not mine.

Where you invest those dollars is up to you. In the section about Investments I'll be sharing more about how common investments work. Don't worry right now about which investments you allocate your investable dollars toward. The idea here is simply to recognize that you have excess cash that isn't working for you.

Retirement Income Planning

In this last section of the Budget & Retirement template we are going to look at how much money you will need to have set aside for retirement. By the way, this isn't the last template in the book.

To figure out how much money you will need to have at retirement depends on multiple factors. So, this tab is going to require some inputs from you. Exactly five inputs, including:

1) Your current age.
2) The age you want to be at retirement.

3) Your annual income goal at retirement. For example, you might want to replace your current income or even aim for having a higher income.
4) We will adjust for inflation. Remember the lesson about inflation eating away at the value of your money? I am assuming an inflation rate of 3%, during your lifetime. Which is currently historically accurate.
5) How much of an annual dividend you can earn. This is one input that will vary depending on the economic environment at the time you are completing this tab. I feel confident that I can earn 5% per year on my money. But, I also have a lot of experience with investing and have a track record of earning more with the investments I handle. If you want to be more conservative use something like 3% as your benchmark.

There is one particular nuance to how I have set up this tab. It assumes that you don't want to touch the principal of your investments, ever, because your goal is to pass all of that money down to your family, friends, charities, etc. That means you will only be spending the interest you earn during retirement.

If passing along all of your principal isn't your goal, or if you will need to draw on your principal to fund your retirement, let me show you a different, easy way to calculate that right now. This used to be called the 4% rule. Which stood for the idea that you could withdraw 4% per year from your investments. In today's environment it is probably closer to 3%. To use this method, simply take the amount of monthly expenses you think you will have during retirement (this is often less for people because they aren't paying for children, hopefully have their debts paid off, etc.) and divide by the percentage you settle on. For example, in retirement you think you will have $4,000 per month in expenses divided by 3%. That means you will need $1.6M (48,000/.03) at retirement.

Section Wrap-up

If you have stuck with me this far, then you should have a pretty good picture of your financial position. Don't panic if it isn't looking as good as you'd like. There are things you can do. There is still time left. The good news is that you now know what you are up against. Whereas most people don't have a real picture of just how close to the proverbial financial cliff that they are.

Now that we have you more aware of your financial state, it's time to go deeper on some subjects. I have brushed over these to this point because I didn't want you distracted with decisions. I simply wanted you to get to an understanding of how things stand.

Next up, I'm going to talk about debt, my personal philosophies, how the most common types of debt work, and share some scenarios that you can use to guide your decision-making.

Debt

The United States has an unhealthy relationship with debt. Let me share a few data points with you to prove it.

First, let's start with the total U.S. debt, which sits at around $34T per the Treasury. Our gross domestic product (GDP), which is the equivalent of income in a personal budget, is expected to be about $26T.

The interest payments on the $34T in debt is $659B per year! I don't like to be political. But, I am going to pause here and encourage you to research more about our country's financial position and ask yourself if it is healthy. If the answer is no, and it should be, then please consider voting for candidates that are open to pushing towards less spending.

Now, let's take a look at individual debt. The below chart, from FRBNY Consumer Credit Panel/Equifax, shows household debt in the U.S. Which just hit an all-time high of $14T. The scary thing is that even through a period where the U.S. government funneled $7T in stimulus into the economy, Americans still borrowed record amounts of debt.

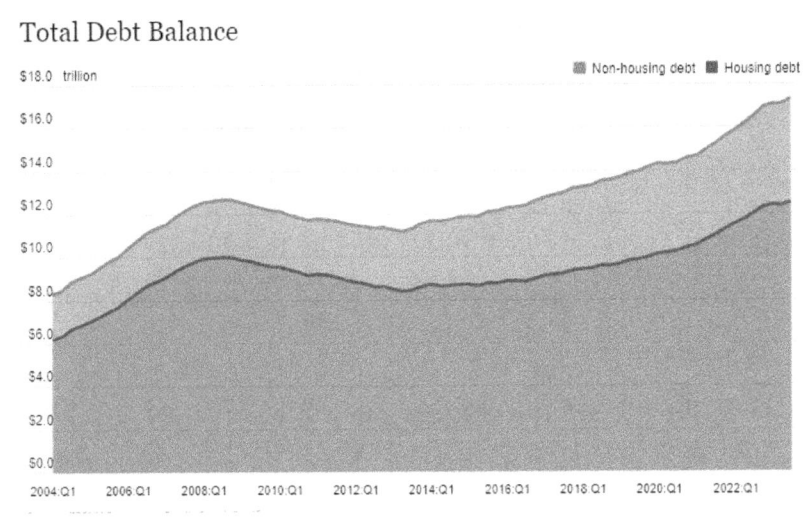

I'm going to stay on my soapbox for just a few more sentences and then I'll move on. There are some people that believe there is such a thing as good debt. Dave Ramsey, a popular financial advice figure, recently took some online heat when he said he would not borrow a billion dollars at 0% interest. Those that mocked him did so because they felt you could borrow that money, invest it in low-risk U.S. Treasuries and earn 5%, effectively free money.

I sit in the middle of the debt argument. I agree with people like Mr. Ramsey that debt is not a good thing. I've just seen so many people struggling to dig themselves out of too much debt, and that can be completely stifling. I've seen marriages end, between people who actually care for each other, simply because they let their financial position get out of control and it caused too much stress in the marriage. On the other hand, I understand the argument that you can leverage debt to make money. For example, borrowing money at 5% interest to invest in real estate that yields a 20% cash-on-cash return.

It is unrealistic to sit up here on my proverbial high-horse and tell you to never have any debt. If you are the super disciplined type that can pull that off that is wonderful. However, the reality is that most people in the U.S. use debt to subsidize their lifestyle.

Instead, I'm going to ask you to be highly conservative with the debt you take on. For example, don't buy a house where the house payment, and associated expenses, will leave you "house broke". Don't run up credit card debt to buy things that you don't really need.

With that, let's move on to the various types of debt and how they work.

Common Debt Terms

There are probably going to be a few phrases or terms that I use across the next few sections, so I want to take a moment and level set on what those are and what they mean. Some of these are super rudimentary. So, if you know them, then just skip ahead to the next section.

Principal = the amount of debt borrowed. This phrase can be confusing because it is used in different ways. Sometimes the principal is not the original loan amount, but the balance of the loan at the moment.

Stress Free Finances

Outstanding balance = I use this phrase to point out the amount of debt owed at the moment. As you make payments, as long as you are paying more than the interest due, you will be reducing the principal owed resulting in an outstanding balance.

Interest = the dollar amount owed to the lender for the debt. You get this through a

Interest rate = the percentage you will pay for having the debt. Ex. 5%. Interest rates are a representation of the risk the lender feels they are taking with your loan. A higher risk loan will have a higher interest rate tied to it.

Fixed interest rate = an interest rate that is set for a specific period of time. Fixed interest rates are most common with larger debts, such as cars and homes.

Variable interest rate = an interest rate that can move up, and sometimes down, based on the amount of the underlying index, such as the Prime rate. As the Prime rate fluctuates, so do variable interest rate loans. You will see this most often with credit cards and Home Equity Lines of Credit (HELOCs).

Term = how long you have to pay back the loan. The loan term also determines how long a fixed interest rate is guaranteed for.

Amortization = this is the fancy accounting term. For now, just think of it as how your payments are scheduled out. In most instances the term and amortization match, but sometimes they don't. Like in adjustable rate mortgages. Ex. a 5/15 mortgage has a 5-year term and a 15-year amortization. You are guaranteed your rate for five years but your payment is broken up over fifteen years.

Payment = this is the amount of money that you have to pay back to the lender at a set interval, usually monthly. It is usually made up of some portion of the payment going to the principal and some towards the interest due. There are loans that we will talk about where most, or even all, of your payment may go towards only satisfying the interest due. It is calculated by a factoring in the principal, interest rate, and time to repay the full amount.

Balloon payment = a large payment that is typically due towards the end of the loan.

Revolving debt = debt that can be reused after you have repaid some of the principal.

Debt-to-Income (DTI) = the percentage of your income that goes towards paying monthly debt payments. Lower is better. If your DTI is 40%, that means that 40% of your income is going towards paying down debts, this includes the proposed new loan. That leaves you with 60% of your income for other, non-debt related expenses.

Loan-to-Value (LTV) = measures the amount of debt that is taken up by an assets value. Lower is better.

How Debt Gets Approved

I can't just educate you on the types of debt, how they work, and their pitfalls. **I want you to understand how lenders think**

about debt in the first place. Not only will that help you make better decisions about the debt you do/don't take on, but it will also help you negotiate more favorable terms.

The first thing to remember is that a lender makes a loan with the expectation of getting paid back. A typical lender will have a default ratio that is less than five percent, sometimes even less than one percent. That is why the lending business can be so profitable, if you know what you are doing.

For almost every loan, you can count on your credit score being a factor. Credit scores have been around for decades and stand-in as a quick and easy way to evaluate a person's ability to repay a loan. More on that in the next section.

Beyond credit scores, lenders look at a variety of other criteria, which can vary based on the type of loan.

Lenders are focused on what is called sources of repayment. Of which there are multiple. **The first source of repayment is your income**. The money you make is used to make the monthly payment on the debt. Lenders will calculate your debt-to-income (DTI). I've added a DTI calculator to the first template, the Budget and Retirement Planning spreadsheet. You can head there to see your DTI. The DTI a lender will allow usually varies based on your credit score and if they have any collateral. Note that a lower DTI is best. That said, a typical top-end that a lender might allow is 50%, with between 40-49% being acceptable, and anything under 30% is good.

The second source of repayment, on some types of loans, is the liquidation of collateral, through repossessing your car or foreclosing on your house. In most instances, lenders will try to avoid liquidating any collateral. Because it is likely that they won't get the full value of the asset. That is why some assets aren't allowed to have a 100% loan-to-value, although it is common on cars to have an LTV higher than 100%.

The final source of repayment is your personal guarantee. Every time you sign a loan agreement you are agreeing that the lender can force you, legally, to repay the loan through other means, such as garnishing your wages, etc.

To tie all of this together, since I mentioned negotiating better terms, if you have a really low DTI and a low LTV, then you should be getting a lower rate than someone who does not. Conversely, if you have a bad credit score with a history of late payments and other issues, then you should expect to have a higher interest rate.

The Basics of Credit Reporting

At one point in my career I sat on a Board of Advisors for one of the three main credit bureaus (Equifax, Experian, and TransUnion). These are the companies that most lenders use to pull your credit information from. In some instances, lenders will use what is called a tri-merge, which is just a merged report from all three lenders.

To be able to access credit bureau information, lenders have to agree to also report their own data. This is not a federal or state law, it is simply part of the operating agreement between the bureau and the lender. For example, if you have a late payment your lender will report that to the bureau(s) that they pull from.

Today, virtually all loans are captured by the bureaus. Even non-traditional types of loans can affect your credit score. Anytime someone sells you something that you are allowed to pay for overtime they are essentially acting like a lender. A great example is if you financed your iPhone. Apple is essentially lending you that phone and collecting the cost of that phone over time. If you failed to make your payments Apple will report you to a credit bureau. Other examples of non-traditional data that is often collected in alternative credit scores include rent and utility payments.

Being on a Board of Advisors for one of the big three gave me an inside look at how the credit bureaus think. I also got a deeper grasp of how their scoring models work. **Each of the three credit bureaus has their own proprietary scoring algorithm where the end score can vary some**. That said, the following is the best way to think about the overall health of your credit score.

- The highest possible credit score you can have is 850.
- The lowest is a 300.
- Here's one word to summarize your credit health based on the score:

- 800+ = Exceptional
- 740-799 = Very good
- 670-739 = Good
- 580-669 = Fair
- <580 = Poor

The things I'm about to share, that impact your credit score, are generalizations across all three of the bureaus. They are not in any particular order. I would encourage you to think of these as levers you can pull to manipulate your credit score up.

- Utilization = I listed this factor first because it can have an out-sized impact on your score. Utilization refers to the percentage of your available balance that you owe. For example, if a credit card company gave you a card with a $10k credit limit and you consistently owe them $9k then your utilization is 90%.
- Credit mix = the types of loans you have affect your credit score. If you have twenty credit card loans that are looked less favorably upon than a credit card, an auto loan, and a mortgage.
- New credit = the older a loan is the more it will help your credit score. New loans, conversely, hurt your credit score. Even worse is when you take out multiple loans in a short amount of time. I've seen this a lot with people who buy a new house. I can't recall the source, but I once heard that 43% of new home owners buy a new car within six months of moving in.

- Too little credit = having little or no credit causes a low score. Why? Because the more you borrower the more data there is to analyze to predict whether or not you will pay back that loan.
- Closed accounts = closing an account can hurt your credit score. Why? Again, that means there is less data for the bureau to use in predicting your ability to pay back other loans.
- Too many applications = even if you don't accept a loan from a lender, the inquiry that they do at the time of application can impact your score. **It is important to note however, that the impact to your score is negligible when multiple inquiries come from the same types of lenders**. For example, most people know that inquiries can impact your score. But the algorithms are smart enough to know when five inquiries come in from car dealership lots (ex. Ford, Toyota, etc.)
- Payment history = making payments on time and consistently is one of the best ways to improve your credit score.
- Late payments = when you fail to make payment on time it negatively impacts your score. If you frequently miss payments it hurts even more. Late payments are tracked in intervals of 30 days. **In most instances, your payment is not reported as late until it is AT LEAST 30 days past due.**

- Bankruptcy = depending on the type of bankruptcy, these stay on your credit for up to ten years. It will impact your credit score less if, as part of the court-approved bankruptcy plan, you paid back some of the money you owed. Having a bankruptcy on your credit is a big hit to the score.
- Foreclosures = these sit around for seven years on your credit. Having a foreclosure on your credit is a big hit to the score.
- Co-signed loans = if you have guaranteed a loan for someone else, that loan will appear on your personal credit and will affect your credit score. My personal stance is that I never co-sign for a loan for anyone that doesn't live in my house and have my last name.
- Business loans = if you personally guaranteed a business loan, which is common, then it can impact your score. Even if the business is a legal entity, ex. LLC, and was the borrower.
- Hard versus soft pulls = A hard pull occurs when you are officially applying for a loan. A soft pull is a way for a lender to assess your credit without the full effects of a hard pull impacting your credit score. Soft pulls are often done for pre-approvals of loans or when you are just shopping for a car and want an idea of what your rate will be.

I hope you are seeing that in some instances, credit scores work in a way that doesn't make sense to you as the borrower. That's the point. **The scoring methods were built to help lenders, who make money making loans, predict if you can and will pay them back.**

You can get a free copy of your credit, annually, from FreeCreditReport.com. I would encourage you to check it regularly and dispute any errors you see. Just be sure you can demonstrate that they are errors. That means you have documentable proof, not just your word.

Your credit score is very important to your financial health because it affects your costs for borrowing money. If you have credit problems, I highly recommend working with a qualified company to improve your credit rating.

Credit Cards

If there is one type of debt I want you to avoid, its credit cards. There is no type of debt with as high a borrowing cost i.e. interest, as credit cards. With payday loans as the exception.

Interest rates are governed at the state level through usury laws. Those laws set the maximum percentage of interest you can be charged. Even with state oversight, the interest on credit cards can be very expensive. The average interest rate at the moment is over 27%! The other thing to be aware of is credit card interest rates are variable. Meaning, they change as rates change when economic factors cause their underlying rates to change. That means they can up. I see this most often with introductory rates on credit cards. The card issuers will offer people an enticing deal, such as 0% for the first three months, to get you to use their card. The next thing you know, you were undisciplined with the card, racked up a big balance, and now the interest rate is more than 20%.

Credit cards are revolving debt. That means that you can use any amount of the approved amount once you pay it back. Here's how that looks.

- You are approved for $10k.
- You owe $2k (outstanding balance)
- So, you have $8k you can still use (available balance)
- You hustled hard this month and have an extra $1k you can pay towards the outstanding balance. You now owe $1k. The $1k you just paid back can now be reused. That is how a revolving debt works.

It's the revolving debt feature that gets people in trouble. They use a credit card for a $1k vacation and then only pay that $1k back in small amounts, like the minimum monthly payment. That minimum monthly payment, often calculated as somewhere between 1%-3% of the balance, is typically not enough of a payment to pay off the interest you were charged last month. Which means, now you are paying interest on the interest you were charged!

Credit cards are particularly dangerous for people early in their financial lives. One of the most common approaches for building a credit profile is when a young adult opens their first credit card(s). What I've seen, in many instances, is that this approach has an inverse effect. The young borrower runs up a balance and struggles to pay that balance down. That's called high utilization, which negatively impacts their credit score.

Below is a template you can use to see the impact of carrying a credit card balance or calculate the cost of a purchase you want to make. I found it online, published by the folks from TheBalance.com.

Type	Description	Link to Content
Credit Card Payment Calculator	You can use this template to calculate the impact of various card balances, interest rates, and payments.	Head here.

I have one exception about the use of credit cards. My family uses a credit card to pay for virtually everything. Because the card we have allows us to build up reward points that we then cash in and use on our annual vacation. We've done this for ten plus years now. Every single month, without fail, I pay the credit card off. Let me be clear, there is danger in this approach. An undisciplined person or someone who goes through a tough financial patch could use this approach and then find themselves carrying over a balance. This approach works for us because I have more than enough money in savings where I can pay off the card if we had a bad month without dipping into our emergency fund.

Summary of key points

- Credit cards typically have very high interest rates.
- Credit cards are usually revolving debt, which means the debt is reusable.
- Where most people get themselves in debt trouble is with credit cards.
- If you only pay the minimum payment you are not paying down your principal and could be paying interest on your interest.
- If you are going to have a credit card that you use for rewards points, make sure you are disciplined enough to pay it off in full every month.

Vehicle loans

Who doesn't love a good looking vehicle? There is something about owning a nice car that makes a person feel special. The type of car a person drives is very much tied to status, particularly in the United States. Therein lies the problem.

There are a few things that have been happening with vehicle loans that make them financial death traps. The cost of cars has risen significantly over time. Some of that has been driven by the amount of technology that is now included in a vehicle. Some of that comes from increasing labor costs, including labor unions pushing for more and more pay. It isn't just the cost of the vehicle that has been on the rise, the total cost of ownership has been going up.

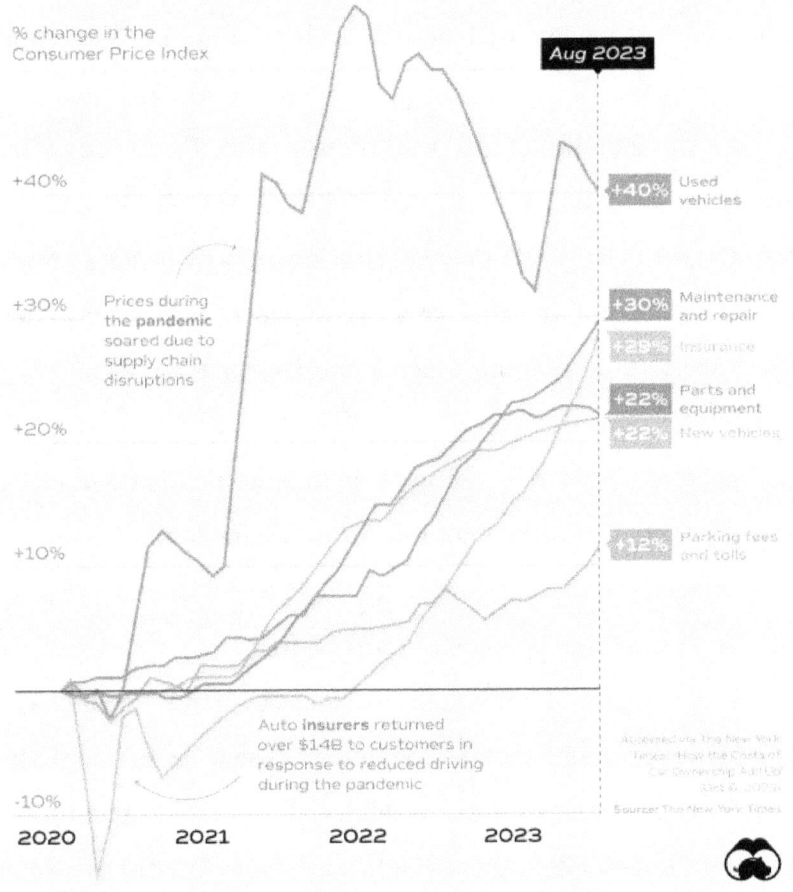

The above image, from the Visual Capitalist, shows that new vehicle prices are up 22%, in just four years, and used prices are up 40%! Insurance is up 29% and maintenance up 30%. According to Consumer Reports, the average price is now over $48,000, with new car payments averaging $726/month and used at $533, per Nerd Wallet. That's just the payment!

The other reason vehicle loans have become so dangerous is that lenders are allowing borrowers to finance vehicles for longer. When I was growing up, the typical car loan was for 48-60 months. Most lenders will now do car loans for up to 84 months, or seven years.

All of that adds up to a position where borrowers are often upside down in their vehicle's equity. Meaning, they owe more than the car is worth. **If there is anything that you take away from this section, it's that cars are depreciating assets**. **They lose value**, unlike a home which is more often than not an appreciating asset.

There are plenty of resources on the internet that will teach you how to buy a car and not fall for the dealership's shenanigans. I'm here to help you make good decisions when buying a car so that you can live stress-free.

That said, I will tell you that I never negotiate the purchase of a car based on the monthly payment. **I focus on the "out-the-door" price. Doing that keeps dealers from tacking on fees**.

Your out-the-door price is a factor of multiple things. Items in red text reduce your out-the-door price.

- the cost of the vehicle, including fees the dealer may try to charge you

Stress Free Finances

- if you put in a down payment. Dealers will prefer this because they know it vastly improves your chances of getting approved.

- any dealership cash incentives.

- your trade-in, which includes:

- the value of the trade-in. If it is more than what you owe. Which you can check on [Kelley Blue Book](#) or [NADA](#). Which is driven based on where you live.

- *less* how much you owe on the trade-in

- your local sales tax

- title and registration fees

- any additional insurance that you buy from dealer such as gap coverage

- care packages (such as prepaid oil changes, paint protection, etc.)

- window tint done at the dealership

- recurring car wash services

- warranties

The scary thing is that the list probably isn't exhaustive. As you can tell, dealerships have figured all kinds of additional revenue streams. In fact, in some instances, the dealerships make more money from other services than from the profit off the vehicle itself. Some [sources](#) list the average profit for selling a car at 4%. So, on a $48k sale the dealership is making less than $2,000. Whereas on warranties and other services, like pre-paid car care services (which I don't recommend), the dealership can profit upwards of 50%.

Then there is the credit spread profit that dealerships can earn. Many dealerships, especially the larger vehicle manufacturers, will self-finance your car loan. More often than not, what they are offering is a lower interest rate but for a lesser amount of time, ex. 1.9% for 60 months. Dealerships also participate in what is called indirect lending programs. These programs are where lenders, including your local bank and credit union, agree to finance the sale of cars that the dealership has. Some of those lenders allow the dealership to mark-up the interest rate. In fact, some statistics say that 78% of car financing includes interest rate mark-up. For example, the lender may approve the loan at 6.5% interest but the dealership's finance & insurance person (F&I) may tell you the rate they approved is 8%. If you accept, they are making 1.5% on just the loan. On an average of a $48k vehicle, that's $720 in extra profit for the dealership and even worse, $720 in extra money you just spent that you didn't need to.

I've worked at both banks and credit unions. At my credit union I was the Chief Lending Officer and oversaw our indirect lending program. We did not allow interest-rate markups. Which is why I am a big fan of credit unions. **I always recommend getting pre-approved for a car loan, before you walk on the dealer lots, so that you can't be duped by extra costs or fees**. Just about any lender will do that for you. Many will even give

Stress Free Finances

you a check in the amount of the pre-approval to use at the dealership.

Let's go back to how car loans are calculated.

Again, there are plenty of resources on the internet. So, I'm going to point you towards my favorite car loan calculator. Although it takes into account things such as sales tax and title and registration, you will need to think through all the other things. Just add them into the amount you put in the Auto Price field.

Type	Description	Link to Content
Auto Loan Calculator	This will take your inputs and come up with your monthly payment. You can switch from the Total Price tab to the Monthly Payment tab to use the payment you can afford and back into the price of a vehicle you can afford.	Head here.

What about leasing a car? I don't recommend it. Leasing can be enticing because lease payments are often lower than loan payments. Which allows people to afford a more expensive car than they might normally qualify for. Plus, many dealership leases come with free maintenance. So, for example, no worrying about your tires needing replacing. Still, in general, leasing is not a good choice. There are a few reasons.

1) In a lease you are the one paying for all the early depreciation that occurs with a car. Have you ever heard the idea that car values drop the second you drive them off the lot? That's the early depreciation. Side note - which is why it's generally recommended that you buy a used car that is between 2-3 years old.
2) When you lease there is never an option of paying off a car and having no payment. Unless you buyout the lease which is crazy expensive.
3) Finally, leases come with restrictive mileage rules where you will be charged hefty fees if you go over those limits.

Then there are recreational vehicle loans. Things like boats, RVs, 4-wheelers, and the like. These all work just like car loans. With one notable exception. Since they are all considered riskier loans the interest rate on those types of vehicles is higher than a traditional car or SUV. For RVs, because of their cost, the term may be longer, ex. 120 months.

Summary of key points

- Cars are depreciating assets. Meaning you will most likely lose money on them.
- Focus on the out-the-door cost of the vehicle, not the monthly payment.

- Get pre-approved for a car loan, with a friendly local lender, like a credit union, before you walk on a dealership lot, to avoid mark-ups and fees.
- I generally recommend no more than 10% of your take home income should go towards a vehicle payment.

Mortgage loans

I need to remind you that my goal here is not to write a book on mortgage loans. What I love about the finance industry is that you can be in it for 20+ years and still have things to learn. Each area of finance is so vast that you can never learn everything there is to know. That's why people focus on specific areas. That said, one of the many departments that reported to me at my bank was the mortgage team.

So, while I won't be going deep into every type of mortgage, I'll focus on sharing the basics, plus how I think about mortgages, so that you have financial peace of mind.

Owning a home has often been called the great American dream. However, in the current economic environment, home ownership is on the decline. According to the National Association of Home Builders, there has been a 3.5% dip from the peak in 2004, to 65.7%, which is below the 25-year average. This dip is largely driven by high interest rates. However, there is some degree of a movement amongst younger people to rent so that they have more mobility and less home maintenance responsibilities.

There are also people, on the internet, who are promoting that it is better to rent than own a home. I'm not here to argue either side. **What I will tell you is that owning a home is not just about the mortgage payment.** Let's take a look at all the costs you need to consider when owning a home.

- The mortgage payment itself, made up of:
    - Principal
    - Interest
    - Insurance; tip - call you auto insurance agent and ask for a quote. Just send them the address of the home you are considering buying.
    - Taxes; tip - you can see the annual tax costs on Realtor and Zillow listings
    - Private Mortgage Insurance (PMI; this is when your loan-to-value is over 80%). PMI is generally a % of your total loan payment and from my experience costs between an additional $100-$250 dollars per month.

Type	Description	Link to content
Mortgage loan estimator	This is my favorite mortgage loan payment	Head here.

Stress Free Finances

Type	Description	Link to content
	calculator, that will include all of the costs I mentioned.	

- Home-owner's Association (HOA) fees if you live in a planned neighborhood
- Trash pickup; may be included in your HOA
- Utilities
    - Water (not just your main water bill, also a sprinkler system if you have one)
    - Electricity
    - Gas
- Decor (the cost of furniture, fixtures, etc.; this can be on-going if you are the type that likes to regularly update things or shop)
- Maintenance and repairs on everything ranging from plumbing, to your air-conditioning, to appliances, and more.
- Renovations (either at the time of purchase or later on)

I could keep going, but I think you get my point. When you buy a home you aren't just taking on a mortgage payment, you are taking on a laundry list of other expenses that you need to account for.

Stress Free Finances

Let's go back to your mortgage payment. **The general rule around mortgage payments is the "28/36" rule**, which means that your mortgage payment shouldn't be more than 28% of your gross monthly income or 36%, with all housing costs included. So, if you earn $100k per year, your mortgage payment should be no more than $2,800.

My stance is that the 28/36 rule is not where you should aim to be. Why? Because the cost of everything is so high right now. My mortgage payment is currently 10% of my gross monthly take home. Why am I sharing? Because that is one reason I live a stress-free financial life. Over the past five years or so we have regularly discussed moving. But every time the thought of being house broke stops us. Could we afford a lot more? Absolutely. Are we willing to stretch ourselves when we already have a great home? Nope.

What's even scarier, and where a lot of people get themselves into trouble, is that mortgage companies, depending on your credit, will approve you for a mortgage payment that is up to 45%, and sometimes more, of your gross monthly income. Can you imagine making $10k per month and your mortgage payment, without all the other expenses, being $4,500!?

So, what do I recommend that I believe most people can live with? **I would target less than 25%, and preferably 20%**. This leaves you buffer for other debts, if you have them, and expenses that you have or that you add (i.e. having a child).

Stress Free Finances

In terms of how mortgage loans work, they are much like any other debt (revisit How Debt Gets Approved). As a recap, lenders will use your credit score and history, calculate your debt-to-income, and compare the value of the home to the loan amount (loan-to-value). All of which I've already covered.

One of the biggest differences is that you should expect to be required to put money down. How much varies on the type of mortgage you can qualify for. For example, First Time Buyer loan programs, through the FHA, have lower down payment requirements (currently 3.5% with a 580 credit score or higher), and lower interest rates. Also, if you expect your down payment to come via a gift that money may need to be "seasoned." Meaning it is in your account for a period of time *prior* to when you will close on your new mortgage.

By the way, one mistake a lot of people make is taking out other debts during or shortly after closing on a new home. When you are in the middle of applying for a new mortgage you should NOT be applying for other debts. Full stop.

For most people, buying a home will be their single largest purchase/expense ever. Will you make money if all goes well and the house appreciates in value? Yes. Will that appreciation be more than if you invested the same amount of money into other investments? Sometimes yes, sometimes no. If you want to buy a house, buy it because you want it and you can afford it. But, don't justify buying a more expensive home than you can reasonable afford by calling it an investment.

Summary of key points
- Focus on the total cost of ownership of a home. Consider ALL of the expenses that you will incur.
- You should expect to put between 3.5-10% down to buy a home. If you put less than 20% down your loan will include PMI.
- Get pre-approved for a mortgage loan before you go house shopping. That way you only look at houses you know you can get approved for. Plus, your realtor will appreciate that, and some even require it to work with buyers.
- I generally recommend no more than 25% of your take home income should go towards a mortgage payment.

Student loans

I was fortunate that my grandparents and parents planned ahead for my college education. So, I didn't need any student loans. When I got my Masters, at the ripe age of 47, my work paid for most of it and the rest I paid for out of our discretionary income. While I'm proud that I got my Masters, with a 4.0 GPA, by the time I got it I had been in the workforce long enough and with a lot of success that it did zero for my career. Zero.

My wife, on the other hand, worked three jobs just to put herself through college. The only student debt she took on was to get an advanced degree that lead her to working in genetics. That debt took us a very long time to pay off.

Stress Free Finances

I'm going to take a moment and share my personal thoughts with you undergraduate and graduate educations. I believe a college education does make a difference in a person's earning power. However, I also believe that some people are not cut out for college, may not want to go to college, or will waste a lot of money going to college and then pick a field that either doesn't interest them or the degree they earn doesn't increase their earning power enough. I also believe that the cost of many programs are overpriced.

Student loans are the one type of loan that I did not get a lot of exposure to in my career. The credit union where I was Chief Lending Officer had evolved out of a college university, yet we still choose not to be involved in student lending due to the complexity.

To avoid pointing you in the wrong direction, but hopefully still provide you some valuable insights, I may point you to a lot of outside resources.

To get us started, student loans are offered by the U.S. federal government, state governments, and private lenders. These loans focus on covering tuition, room, and board. However, they can be used for other living expenses such as rent, food, school supplies, etc.

The amount you can borrow is based on each school's cost of attendance (COA). Lenders do not track your expenses. They simply approve you for a loan amount, fund that loan, and then expect you to pay it back.

Payback of a student loan works like any other unsecured loan. Meaning you won't need to put up any collateral. You are just expected to make recurring payments. Where you need to be careful is when repayment is deferred for a period of time, whether because the lender is allowing you to wait to make payments until after your schooling is over or because you request a deferment yourself. Either way, be aware that interest could still be accruing.

Student loans are approved based on a variety of factors. Here's a link that outlines the requirements for federal financial aid. Federal loans require you to prove you need financial assistance. There is no set amount of income, but know that if your or your family's income is too high you could be denied a federal student loan. Private student loans are more about creditworthiness, which I've discussed in general earlier.

The way I want you to think about student loans is as an investment. If the education and degree you will receive doesn't earn you a reasonable salary that can earn you a strong return over time then it may not be worth the cost. To help you figure that out, I found a great article where the author(s) calculated the return on investment (ROI) of over 30,000 college degrees from a variety of colleges. You can check it out below.

Stress Free Finances

File	Description	Status
Federal Student Loan Aid requirements	Outlines the requirements to be eligible for federal student loan aid. Includes a link to the Free Application for Federal Student Aid form.	Head here.
Bachelor's degree ROI database	The Foundation for Research on Equal Opportunity's article on college degree ROIs.	Head here.

Summary of key points
- There are two types of student loans - federal and private.
- These loans act a lot like unsecured loans, that I talked about earlier.
- In many instances you can delay repayment of your student loan until you are out of school.
- Think about student loans as an investment. Is the education you are getting, and the job opportunities that should lead you to, worth the amount of money you may need to borrow?

Debt snowballing

I struggled with where to put this section. You could argue that it belongs in the budgeting section. But, since it is all about debt, I'm dropping it here after we've talked through how each debt works.

Having a lot of debt is one of the quickest ways to NOT live stress-free. The best defense is to not take on a lot of unnecessary debt in the first place. But, if you have a lot of debt and are wondering which debts to pay off first you should consider the debt snowball approach.

The idea of debt snowballing is a framework where you pay off debts off strategically based on a the balance off each debt, the interest rate, and the time it would take you to eliminate each debt based on your discretionary income.

As a reminder, the two best things you can do to move towards eliminating your debts are creating additional income and building and sticking to a budget.

One of the easiest ways to create a debt snowball plan is to use software to help you in your decisions about which debt to attack first. I recommend either Schwab's Debt Elimination Calculator or, if you are a follower of his method, the Dave Ramsey Debt Snowball Calculator. Links to both are below.

File	Description	Status
Debt Elimination Calculator	Schwab's version	Head here.
Debt Snowball Calculator	Dave Ramsey's version	Head here.

Ramsey tends to have people focus on paying off the smallest debts first. I like that idea because it helps to create some momentum by allowing people to see early progress. When you are trying to chew down a $15,000 debt by paying an extra $500 per month, it's going to be a while before it's paid off. Whereas other approaches will have you focus on the debt with the highest interest rate first.

I recommend a combination of the two approaches. Focus on paying off any debts that you can get rid off in less than six months through extra income or tightening your budget. Then take the payments you saved, add them to the extra money you are using to pay down debts, and attack anything that will take longer than six months based on the interest rate followed by smaller balances before larger ones.

Section Wrap-up

I'm not going to rehash all the things I've shared in this section on debt. What I recommend is that you review the appropriate section(s) anytime you are thinking about taking on a new debt.

Instead, what I want to do, one more time, is reinforce the negative role that too much debt can have on your life. Debt is one of, if not the largest, creators of stress in your life. I can say that because I've been there. I spent five years of my life hustling to create additional income so that we could pay off a ton of debt. We still have some to go, our home, but **if you want to know what really allows us to live a stress-free financial life its having paid off almost all of our debt.**

Investments

Some forms of investing have been compared to gambling. It can feel that way if you don't know what you are doing. But, there is a difference between pure speculation, which is what many people are participating in by doing no research and investing based on a feeling or someone else's opinion, and intelligently investing your hard-earned money.

The good news is that you can do the latter, intelligently invest your money, by learning the basics. You don't need to understand credit swaps, hedging, or even options trading to earn a consistently good yield. That said, I feel compelled to point out that markets are volatile and can be unpredictable. There are factors you can't control and sometimes can't even anticipate that can affect your results. So, you should expect to have periods where your investments may lose money. But, altogether, if you invest wisely, you should have a net-positive gain over an extended period of time. For example, out of the last fifteen years, the S&P 500 index was down only two times.

Before I dive into specific investment options and tips, I want to spend some time setting a foundation for your investing activities, including some fundamentals, best practices, and other things to consider. Then we will get into specific investments.

Investment Fundamentals

I've learned over the years that I am a teacher at heart. When I teach someone a new topic I focus on the basics, because that is often all they need to master to be successful. The same is true for investing. Grasping the basics, deeply, is more than enough to lead you to an outsized positive result with your investing activities.

How much should you be investing?

I hate to tell you this, but there is no magic number for how much you should be investing. That's because it all depends on where you are in your financial journey. If you are barely making it by each month, then the amount you budget for investing will be less than someone who has more discretionary income.

That said, **I recommend investing at least a little bit each month**. Is that my recommendation even if you have a ton of debt that needs to be paid off? Yes. Why? Because, the earlier you start investing the more time you have to take advantage of compounding interest, and investing early will help solidify investing as a habit. **This is so important - even small amounts of investing, whatever you can do, add up over time.**

The way I want you to address how much you should be investing is to revisit the Investable Dollar portion of your budget spreadsheet. If you have more than your target emergency fund built up in cash, you should consider putting that money to work. Now, that only accounts for chunks of cash you could be investing. Next, head back to the Budget Forecasting part of the Budget worksheet, scroll down to the Investments section, and let's enter an amount for how much you feel like you can carve out each month to invest. It doesn't matter if it's as low as $25 or $50, the goal here is to see the impact this has on your budget and if you can make it work. If your budget still looks ok, then experiment with a higher number. Keep raising your monthly investment amount until it gets close to being uncomfortable. **If you are looking for a benchmark, target 15% of your take home pay as a solid goal to aim for with your investing.** Notice that I said your take home pay, not your gross pay before deductions.

Financial goals

"With one eye on the future, there is only one eye left with which to find the way."

I'm a fan of mantras, and the one I just shared is a long-time favorite of mine. Like a lot of people, I have a habit of focusing on the focus. Of looking towards the future and missing out on the next immediate step in front of me that will get me to that future.

As with any goal, including financial goals, if you are constantly focused on near-term results you may be chasing after things that won't get you to your end goal. So, with investing, you need an overarching goal to help guide your strategy. That goal will likely be broken down into sub-themes. For example, your focus might be, on planning for retirement. But, if that timeline is far out, you might be focused on getting out of debt. Fortunately, they work nicely together, even with different timelines, because getting out of debt will allow you to invest more. **The key is that your short-term goals should be leading you down the path toward a longer-term goal.** If not, then you need to realign your goals.

Here's a bad example of goal alignment.

Short-term goal: I want to get a budget established and stick to it so I can build up an emergency fund.

Long-term goal: I want to buy a Lamborghini with my emergency fund.

I like fast cars too, but why would you go through all the effort of making some good financial decisions in the near term to turn around and ruin it with bad decisions later on?

So, take a moment to determine your financial goals. Break them up into short (less than one year to accomplish) and long-term goals (anything that will take longer than one year to accomplish). Here's some common examples of each.

Examples of short-term financial goals

- Save up $1,000
- Save up a specific amount for a particular purchase (maybe a vacation)
- Create a budget and begin sticking to it
- Find a way to increase your income, maybe through a side hustle
- Payoff a small debt that has a high interest rate

- Pay back a loan from a family member or friend
- Downsize the car you have because you bought your monthly payment is too big

Examples of long-term financial goals
- Save up a down payment for a home or an investment property
- Work through the debt snowball method until all of your credit cards are paid off
- Increase your 401(k) contributions by 1% per year
- Build up an education fund for your kid(s) to be able to afford college
- Begin setting money aside for a child's first car (btw - I started saving for our daughter's first car when she was four. A few months ago we bought it and gave it to her. It was a proud moment for us since we had worked towards that goal for 12 years)

Risk vs. return & risk tolerance

All investing contains risk. Even keeping all of your money on the sidelines carries with it the risk of your cash being devalued over time by inflation. When investing, you need to be prepared that your investments could lose some or all of their value. The key is balancing that risk as much as possible. Think of investing like a seesaw. **The riskier an investment, the larger the return you should expect**. But, the greater the chance that you lose everything.

Stress Free Finances

Savings accounts at banks pay a smaller rate of return because it is highly unlikely that you will lose value in that account. Whereas, investors who invest in startups expect double-digit returns because doing so is highly risky.

That is why it is important for you to consider your risk tolerance. Here's an easy way to test your risk tolerance. When you go to make an investment, ask yourself how you would respond if the investment lost 10%, 20%, 50%, 75%, or even all of its value. If you lost 10% in one day would you be tempted to sell the investment and stop the loses? Maybe not. Maybe you'd stand your ground. But, what if it lost 50% overnight?

To gauge your risk tolerance, I'm going to send you to take a quiz. The following is a link to Transamerica's risk tolerance quiz. Me and my team use their products quite a bit, and I like how they break things down.

File	Description	Status
Transamerica's risk tolerance quiz	Scroll down to about the middle of the page and click the button.	Head here.

Once you have the results, go ahead and put save that information somewhere. Every time you think about making an investment, refer back to your risk tolerance category and ask yourself if the investment aligns with your comfort level. If not, you may not want to make the investment. You should also share this information with any financial professional you choose to work with.

Asset allocation

My wife is the queen of moderation. If she wants some ice cream, she only eats one spoonful. She is balanced in virtually all things. You need to be like my wife with your investment portfolio, balanced.

Asset allocation refers to how much of your total investment portfolio is invested in individual categories. Exactly how you allocate your investments will vary based on a lot of factors. Including how long you have until retirement, your risk tolerance, your goals, and more.

Generally speaking, the older you are the more you should have in conservative investment categories such as bonds. That is because you have less time to recover if the markets take a huge dip. If you are younger and have a longer horizon until retirement then you can afford to have your investments in more aggressive investments. Many financial professionals consider a mix of 60% stocks and 40% bonds a balanced portfolio. But, if you have a longer timeframe to retirement it might make more sense to have, say, 75% of your portfolio in stocks and 25% in bonds.

Of course, I've only referred to stocks and bonds. A truly diverse asset allocation would mean having investments in cash, stocks, bonds, real estate, and potentially even cryptocurrency.

I looked for a resource that I felt comfortable sharing with you, but every example that I reviewed didn't feel detailed enough or from a credible enough source. So, if you are managing your own investing, I don't have much to offer in terms of helping you choose an asset allocation model to work under. The good news is, if you work with an advisor or you have access to investment platforms they usually have asset allocation software that will help you figure out a strategy based on the factors I mentioned above.

Rebalancing

There could be times where you end up with too much money invested in one particular asset class. That happens because the value of a particular investment category could outperform others, thereby throwing your asset allocation weights out of whack. When that happens you should rebalance your portfolio.

Rebalancing your investment portfolio is the best way to reset things back to your original asset allocation. I've heard it recommended that you consider rebalancing at least one per year. **To rebalance, you sell assets that are overweight, meaning the amount of value in them has grown well beyond your intended asset allocation, and then buy underweight investments.** Many investment platforms offer software that will help you rebalance your portfolio efficiently.

One thing to consider - **you could incur capital gains taxes along the way**. So, if you are unsure of how to avoid getting a tax bill, check with your accountant or advisor.

Dollar-cost averaging (DCA)

The concept behind dollar-cost averaging involves **investing a fixed amount of money into an investment at consistent intervals**. The main purpose of this strategy is to smooth out the volatility in the chosen investment. Since investment prices fluctuate, if you are occasionally buying when the price is high and occasionally when it is low, then theoretically your average cost per share is lower over time.

There is another benefit, albeit indirect, of using the DCA strategy. The only way to take true advantage of the approach is to invest consistently, periodically over an extended period of time. This is very habit forming and will get you in the habit of making regular investments. If you set this up using an automatic withdrawal from an account then you won't have to think about it and it acts like the pay yourself first budgeting method.

Once again, depending on where you are managing your investments, the platform you are on will likely have a way to automate your DCA activities. Some platforms even allow you to set a timeframe for when you want to execute your DCA and the system will automatically perform the trades and reinvestments within your existing portfolio.

Investment Best Practices

I, ah, didn't know where else to put these topics. So, "Investment Best Practices" it is! Seriously though, the things in this section may feel basic or generic. They are, that's the point. Remember, it's the basics that I want you to get down.

Automating your investments

One of the most powerful financial tools that everyone has at their disposal is the ability to automate your financial activities. From setting up automatic bill payments, to recurring deposits into your savings account, and automating your investment activities.

Just about every modern investing platform will allow you to automatically move money into your investment accounts and even auto allocate that money to specific investments that you elect. So, be sure to take advantage of that technology. There are a lot of benefits to automating your investing. First off, by automating it you reduce that chance that you will spend that money instead of investing it. Second, you reduce decision fatigue when you have that money go into predetermined investments such as individual stocks and/or funds.

One note here, I don't recommend setting up auto investments for the full amount you can afford to invest each month, especially if that pushes your budget to the limit. Because your budget will see ebbs and flows, you could have a higher expense month where a large automatic investment could put you in the negative.

Common mistakes

We've talked about this earlier, related to debt. The most common mistake I see with investing is making investment decisions based on a feeling versus data and information. Fear of missing out, FOMO, is one of the leading causes of bad investment decisions. People get caught up in being in on the next hot investment opportunity and so they invest based on someone else's opinion, which is more times than not unsupported.

Cryptocurrency and meme stocks are good examples. Sure, plenty of people have made money on those investments. But, a lot, maybe even more, lost money because they tried to jump on the bandwagon too late or they held on too long.

So, commit today to only invest money in an opportunity after you have done your own research. If you aren't sure how to evaluate investments, read some articles or take a course. Also, in each section, I'll share some of the ways I personally evaluate each investment class.

Another common mistake is not being a long-term minded investor. I've talked to people who exited an investment after earning a reasonable return, only to regret not sticking with that investment over a longer period of time. A good example is the NVidia stock. Remember, this book was written in the first part of 2024, when that stock has been on a tear. Some investors took their gains early on, only to miss out on the full extent of the gains the stock saw. The flip side is true. Some investors will panic if an investment sees a short-term loss and will pull their money out. Meanwhile, the investment has a correction and they could have recouped some or all of their loss.

Finally, I see a lot of people choose to manage their own investments. While there are plenty of software options to help you do that, the truth is that most people don't have the right amount of knowledge and they definitely don't have the time to sit around and watch their investments all day. If you are going to manage your own investing, I recommend a "set it and forget it" approach where you invest in funds that will earn you a relatively safe rate of return and where you don't need to stay on top of any volatility that may arise.

What I'm trying to impart is that the most common mistakes are all lapse of judgment and come from emotional decision-making. Don't be that investor. What's the best defense? Falling back on data and information.

Fees & costs

Nearly every investment you make will come with a fee or cost. For example, while some platforms allow you to make fee-free trades (Robin hood is a good example of this), others may charge you to buy individual stocks. Other examples of fees include whenever someone else is managing your money for you. Your 401(k) program at work is managed by a firm and they charge you fees to administer that program. It is common to pay 1%, or more, in what is called a managed brokerage account, where a financial advisor actively manages your investments. One more final example - even mutual fund indices charge fees.

The key is to be mindful of the fees you are paying and what you are getting in return for those fees. If you are paying someone 1% to actively manage your investments and the rate of return they have won you isn't beating an average index then you are wasting your money. However, if you are paying a 1% fee in an account and that account is outperforming the average rate of return then it is well worth it.

Let's look at an example. Say you have $100,000 in an investment with a .50% annual fee. Which is a moderate fee. That's $500 per year in fees. Over twenty years, you are losing out on almost $20,000 that you could have been earning on that $500 per year assuming you'd earn 5% in interest.

Some people are adamant that you shouldn't pay any fees on investments. I don't recommend getting overly focused on fees, so long as the return is consistently worth the expense. **The point is to focus on your return, net of fees**. If an investment is consistently earning you 8% per year and it has a 1% fee, you are netting 7% per year. That beats a 5% return with no fees.

Compounding interest & reinvesting

Ok, please pay attention to the next paragraph or so. One of the most powerful financial principles is taking advantage of compounding interest. **Compounding interest is when you earn interest on your interest.** Say what!? How do you do that?

When your investments are producing interest or dividends you have the option to either take those earnings out as income, and possibly pay taxes on that income, or reinvest those earnings back into the account where they came from.

Let's say you have $10,000 of Microsoft stock. Today, July 7th, 2024, the dividend Microsoft is paying is 0.64%. That means you'd get a dividend payout of $64. If you allowed that $64 to be reinvested back into Microsoft stock, which most platforms can do for you automatically, then the next time Microsoft declares a dividend of, for example, the same amount, you'd earn 0.64% on your original $10,000 <u>and</u> the $64 you reinvested. That may not sound like a lot, but over time it can really add up.

I like to think of compounding interest as free money. You didn't have to do anything extra to earn that money, you simply allowed your money to do the work. So, whenever possible, elect to have any interest or dividends you earn reinvested. Most of the time you will want to have that money reinvested right back into the same investment it was paid out from. But, there is nothing stopping you from taking a payout and investing it elsewhere. For example, if you have a significant dividend-paying portfolio, instead of reinvesting that money into the markets you could use those dividends to put down money on a real estate investment. Personally, I like to reinvest earnings right back into the source they came from.

Other Considerations

This section holds a few other topics that I didn't feel belonged anywhere else. It also has some of my strongest opinions, particularly around whether or not you should manage your own money. As always, it is your financial future, not mine. I'm simply sharing my advice and opinion on these topics. If you don't like my advice, don't heed it. Or, go write your own book 😄.

Fractional shares

Today, August 3rd, Class A shares of Berkshire Hathaway stock are selling for $641,435. That is for one share. But, did you know that you can still own some of that stock? How? Through fractional shares.

Think of buying fractional shares of particular stock like buying one slice of an entire pizza. A fractional share is like buying a slice of a company. Let's say you want to invest in Berkshire's Class A stock. But, you only have $50 to invest in it. You can still own $50 worth of that stock. You still get all of the same benefits, such as sharing in the growth of the stock and even earning dividends if the company pays them. Your share of those things is equivalent to the fractional percentage of a single stock that you own. The only big difference is that if you do not at least own a full share in a company, so anything less than one full share, you have no voting rights.

Most investment platforms will let you buy and own fractional shares of stock.

Should you manage your own investments?

I have 25+ years of experience in finance, a great track record with investment decisions, and a few financial licenses. But, I still use another licensed advisor to manage most of my investments. Why? For a few reasons. First, using an independent advisor allows me to make sure I'm not making biased, emotional investment decisions. Second, I don't have the time to analyze and monitor the market on a regular basis.

Now, before you start yelling at me about "set it and forget it" investment options like S&P 500 funds that perform well with no supervision, understand that I use funds like those for a lot of my money. But, I also invest in more aggressive investments and I feel better knowing that our advisor is focused on those things. For me, **it all goes back to the return I'm getting for the fees I'm paying. If my advisor helps me get an overall better return than I can get on my own then it's worth it. Otherwise, sure, manage your own money if you feel like you have the experience, time, and stomach to handle those decisions**.

Also, just to be clear, our advisor manages most of our money. Not all of it. Why? Because I like to trade for fun. So, I keep a separate, small investment account where I make investments on my own. Again, I have lots of experience in this arena and the money in that account is what I consider "light it on fire and watch it burn" money. If I lose money then I lose money. It's money I can afford to lose every bit of.

Some of my favorite resources

Ok, one more section before we get into individual investment options. The wonderful thing about investing in today's market is that there are all kinds of technological advances and resources that make investing easier.

At the risk of getting too complicated, I'm going to list some of my favorite investment resources here, and in the Resources section towards the end of the book.

One note - most of these resources are for people who are managing some, or all, of their own money.

Investment platforms

The investment platform that you choose depends on the variety of investment options that you need. Most platforms will give you the ability to invest in stocks, bonds, mutual funds, etc. Many will allow you to buy and sell options or trade using margin accounts.

The platforms I am going to share are those that I have first-hand experience using. I am NOT getting compensated in any way to share or link to these resources.

TD Ameritrade (acquired by Schwab)

TD Ameritrade was the first platform I used, decades ago, to manage my own investment activities. Early on I bought individual stocks through their platform. Later I added mutual funds, ETFs, and more recently, I house one of my ROTH IRAs there. However, I do not hold any cryptocurrency positions with them, as they don't currently support that in the form of real ownership.

Not only is Schwab a secure company, with $118B in market cap as of 9/29/2024, but they offer a lot in the way of investment options and tools. I have not taken advantage of their educational platform, but from the looks of it, it is fairly robust. **Under the Learn tab they have courses, podcasts, a magazine, a coaching area, a new client welcome center, tools for both technical and fundamental analysis, and more**.

Moving money into and out of their platform is easy and relatively quick.

One upgrade that occurred when Schwab acquired TD Ameritrade is that the user interface (UI) is much cleaner. Ameritrade's was fine, but it wasn't as modern.

Schwab does not charge a fee for online trades of stocks, EFTs, mutual funds, and options. They used to, before Robin hood and other platforms popularized no fee trading. If you use one of their brokers to make a trade then there is a fee.

Robinhood

To be transparent, at the time of writing this, I do not have any money invested through Robin hood's platform. However, I have held tens of thousands of dollars on their platform in the past.

Stress Free Finances

Robin hood gained in popularity during the COVID-19 pandemic. **From a user interface (UI) perspective, their platform is one of the best in my opinion**. Also, Robin hood will give you instant access to trade with some or all of any deposits you make (currently up to $1,000 as of 9/29/2024).

Through their platform you can invest in stocks, including fractional shares, ETFs, options, and limited cryptocurrencies (mostly the mainstream ones). You can also house Traditional and Roth IRAs there. Robin wood also offers cash accounts where, at times, you can earn a higher than normal yield.

One thing I didn't enjoy about buying cryptocurrencies through Robin hood. There has been some debate about whether or not they buy real coins on an investor's behalf or if they are simply making investments and holding shares via a promise to the investor. I dug around and found contrasting opinions about this, so take some time to do your own research.

Coinbase

If you want to invest in cryptocurrencies, this is the platform I use and recommend. Their user interface is strong and intuitive, they offer **one of, if not the largest, selection of coins to invest in**, moving money into and out of their platform is easy, and when you invest via Coin base you own real coins.

Through Coin base you can "stake" your coins and earn a high-yield against those coins. Staking is the process of locking digital tokens in a block chain network to earn rewards and help validate transactions.

Resources for analyzing the economy

I don't recommend trying to read the markets. But, I am a fan of keeping up with what is going on in the macro-economic environment, because that can affect your ability to earn a return on your investments.

There are a few key statistics I like to keep a pulse on, plus a few comments on each data point.

- Inflation
  - You don't want 0%. The Feds target is generally 2%. Too high of inflation and the Fed will raise rates to keep spending down.
- The Consumer Price Index
  - This measures changes in prices by baskets of goods and services. It is the best indicator of inflation. As with inflation, you don't want 0%, because then consumers spend like drunken sailors and inflation eventually rises.
- Unemployment
  - High unemployment is a sign of issues in the economy. A rising unemployment rate is often a signal of tough economic times on the horizon.

- The Fed Funds Rate
  - This rate is the benchmark for almost all other rates. If it is raised then most likely other interest rates will go up as well.
- GDP, or Gross Domestic Product
  - This is a measurement of how the total value of goods and services a country produces. In good economic times, and a stable import/export environment, you want a higher GDP.
- PCE, or Personal Consumption Expenditures
  - This is the largest component of GDP, making up about 70% of it. A higher PCE means consumers are spending more which is usually seen as one sign of a strong economy
- Interest Rates
  - This is really important to understand. High interest rates aren't always bad. Say what!? They are for borrowers, because loan payments are higher. But when interest rates are high, you can expect some investments (ex. savings accounts, certificates) to pay a higher yield.

That may feel like a lot to keep up with. It's not. Because you can get all of it from one resource. That resource is the Federal Reserve Economic Data (FRED) website. Just head there and you will find easy access to all kinds of data points.

Ways I analyze stocks

Don't hate me. I started to include resources in this section and then realized I would be doing you a disservice. Why? Because, in the beginning, I said this book wasn't going to be about day trading, etc. Also, while I have a ton of experience with trading, I don't personally do a lot of technical analysis of the stocks I am interested in.

So, I'm not going to give you links to a bunch of resources for analyzing stocks. Here's what I will do, though. I'll list out the things I look at or think about when deciding if I am going to invest in a company.

- Leadership experience: companies with experienced leadership make me more confident that they can steer the ship to better returns. You can find this information through online searches. I steer clear of companies with high leadership turnover.
- Required reports: I review the company's annual reports (called a 10k) and quarterly reports (10q) to see how they are talking about their past and future expectations. Are they lowering or raising guidance? Which is a fancy way of saying lowering or raising expectations. Are they thinking about the right things? What are they saying about the economy?
- Review competitors: how are they performing? Better or worse? Why?

- Stock buybacks: if a company buys back its own stock that is generally seen as a sign of confidence, since the company is using its own cash to buy back shares.
- Dividends: if the company has a history of paying a dividend, did they reduce it (usually not good; unless they had a lot of capital expenditures)?
- Leadership trading: top leaders in public companies have to disclose if they buy or sell shares in the company. If they are selling that could signal a loss of confidence. Of course, they could be simply diversifying or need the cash.
- Individual stock performance indicators: here are some of things specific to the company or the stock that I look at, of which, many are available to see inside popular trading platforms:
    - Revenue: is it growing? How much compared to competitors?
    - Expenses: is it growing faster than revenue?
    - Both of those will feed to the company's net income performance.
    - P/E ratio: This is the stock's Price-to-Earnings per share. The lower the number the better, which indicates a company that has strong earnings but isn't too expensive to purchase their shares.
    - EPS ratio: This is the Earnings-per-Share. A higher EPS is best.

- 52-week high/low: I look at the 52-week high and low and where the stock price is in the range. If it's at the very top the stock is expensive and may, not that I said may, not have much room to grow. If it's too low, is it on the way down or does that mean it has room to grow?
- Beta: A stock's beta signals its volatility in relation to the rest of the market. Anything below a 1.0 beta is considered safer and over a 1.0 is increased volatility.

I'm going to leave it at that. If you analyze just those aspects of a stock then you are doing far more research than your average investor who is making emotional bets.

Investment Options

Savings accounts

Savings accounts are offered by depository institutions, such as banks and credit unions. Whereas your checking account is where most of your daily transactions occur, a savings account is **usually set aside for some sort of savings goal**, such as building an emergency fund or putting specific monies aside for a big purchase. Today, they are insured by the government for up to $250,000.

Savings accounts will pay you interest, but don't count on it being a lot. Most will pay you between 0.10%-0.50%. There are high-yield savings accounts that pay more. Banks use them to attract deposits that they can lend out to make a return. For example, I have a high-yield account that is paying me 4.00% right now. Banks can change their savings rate at any time.

These accounts are considered liquid, in that you can withdraw your money at any time. However, be aware that up until 2020, Regulation D limited the number of withdrawals and transfers to six per month. Following the COVID-19 pandemic, that was paused.

Certificates of Deposit (CDs)

A CD is like a savings account but the money you deposit is **not eligible for early withdrawal without paying a penalty** against the interest you have earned. That penalty does not affect your original deposit.

These accounts pay higher interest than a savings account because when you deposit the money you are agreeing to leave the money on deposit with the bank for a period of time ranging from months to years. The longer the period of time, the higher the interest rate you can earn. Unlike a savings account, the rate on a CD is guaranteed for the period of time you commit your funds to the bank.

Because they are guaranteed by the bank and insured by the government, CDs are considered low-risk investments.

Right now, today is October 6th, 2024, I am seeing CD rates as high as the 4-5% range.

Treasuries

I **think of Treasuries like Certificates of Deposit, but the money sits with the U.S. government**, not a bank. If you want about as low risk an investment as possible, Treasuries are one of the lowest risks available because they are fully backed by the U.S. government.

There are a few main types of Treasuries:
- T-bills are sold at a discount and don't pay interest. When they mature, from days to up to one-year, you collect the difference between the amount you invested and the discount.
- T-notes have maturities ranging from a few years to 10 years and pay a fixed interest rate.
- T-bonds have 20 or 30 year maturities and also pay a fixed interest rate.

Treasuries have a few other benefits. They can be bought and sold, so they are considered liquid. Also, **interest income from Treasuries is generally not taxed by state and local governments**.

You can buy Treasuries through banks and brokers, or directly from TreasuryDirect.gov, which is what I have used in the past.

Stocks

When you buy a stock, you are investing in the underlying company. For example, if you buy shares of Apple you legitimately own some of the company. That said, you generally do not have any power over the operations of that company unless you are on the Board, have influence because of the amount of shares you own, etc. You may, depending on the types of shares you own, have voting rights related to certain actions, such as Board appointments. But, all told, **your power is limited to the number of shares you have**.

There are two main types of shares you can own. **Common and Preferred shares**. Common shares give you voting privileges, and eligibility to dividends when declared. Preferred shares are more like a hybrid between stocks and bonds because their owners get a fixed dividend payment. Whereas, common shareholders are not guaranteed a dividend, whose payment depends on the performance of the company.

Companies can further classify their shares as Class A or B shares. Class A have more voting rights, but Class B get dividend higher payouts.

When considering investing in stocks, you need to understand that they are generally categorized a few ways:
- Based on market capitalization, i.e. the total value of the company's stock.
    - Large-cap : @$10B or more
    - Mid-cap: @$2B-$10B
    - Small-cap: @$300M-$2B
- By sector - i.e. the industry the company is in. ex. Tech, healthcare, energy
- By location - i.e. domestic or international

- By characteristics:
    - Growth: companies with high grow-rates
    - Value: undervalued companies with a larger price appreciation opportunity
    - Income: companies that pay higher dividends

Bonds

Investing in bonds is like becoming a lender yourself. You are lending your money to a company or government or municipality in exchange for interest payments and possibly appreciation in the bond's value, that can be based on fixed or variable rates, and the promise they will pay you back.

Bonds have a rating system that is meant to symbolize the risk of the bond.

Investment grade:
- AAA/Aja: Highest quality, extremely low risk of default.
- AA/Aa: Very high quality, low risk of default.
- A/A: High quality, slightly higher risk than AA.
- BBB/Baa: Medium quality, moderate risk of default.

Speculative grade (also known as "junk bonds" or "high-yield bonds"):
- BB/Ba: Speculative, substantial risk of default.
- B/B: Highly speculative, high risk of default.
- CCC/CA: Very highly speculative, very high risk of default.

- D/D: In default, payment of interest and/or principal is in arrears.

With most investment portfolios, it is recommended that you mix bonds with stocks because they tend to balance one another out in terms of volatility and/or risk. Also, note that bonds generally have an inverse relationship with interest rates. So, if interest rates are going up, bond prices/yields will be going down.

Mutual Funds & ETFs

Mutual funds and ETFs (exchange-traded funds) are both types of investments that pool money from multiple investors to invest in a diversified portfolio of assets, such as stocks, bonds, or other securities. However, there are some key differences between the two:

Mutual Funds

- **Pricing:** Mutual funds are priced once a day, at the end of the trading day. This means that all investors who buy or sell shares on a given day will receive the same price, known as the net asset value (NAV).
- **Trading:** Mutual funds are bought and sold through the fund company itself, rather than on an exchange. This means that you can typically only buy or sell shares once a day.
- **Management:** Most mutual funds are actively managed, meaning that a fund manager makes decisions about

which securities to buy and sell. This can lead to higher fees, but it can also potentially lead to higher returns.

- **Minimum investment:** Mutual funds often have minimum investment requirements, which can vary depending on the fund.

ETFs

- **Pricing:** ETFs are traded on an exchange, just like stocks. This means that their price fluctuates throughout the day, and you can buy or sell shares at any time during trading hours.
- **Trading:** ETFs are bought and sold through a brokerage account, just like stocks. This means that you can typically buy or sell shares as often as you like.
- **Management:** Most ETFs are passively managed, meaning that they track a specific index, such as the S&P 500. This typically leads to lower fees than actively managed mutual funds.
- **Minimum investment:** ETFs typically do not have minimum investment requirements, although you will need to buy at least one share.

If you are **looking for a low-cost, diversified investment, an ETF may be a good option. If you are looking for a more hands-on approach and are willing to pay higher fees for the potential of higher returns, a mutual fund may be a better choice.**

Retirement Accounts

401(k)

Pension plans, where employees get paid a recurring amount at retirement based on their income and time at a business, aren't very common any more. They were replaced by 401(k), the name of which refers to the tax code the rules come from.

Through a 401(k), your employer encourages you to save for retirement by contributing a fixed amount or a percentage of your income. The employer will then match your contribution up to the amount that they set. Keep in mind that there are limits to how much you can contribute to a 401(k). Those limits can be set by your employer and there are also government limits.

The amount you contribute can be pre-tax (Traditional) or post-tax (Roth). The benefit to pre-tax is that those contributions limit your taxable income, while post-tax means your full income is taxed. **People that prefer Roth accounts do so because they believe that taxes will be higher in the future**.

Good plans come with a variety of investment options in them including cash accounts that pay interest, stocks, mutual funds, REITs, etc.

These accounts do come with early withdrawal challenges. If you pull money out before age 59 and one-half, you will pay a 10% penalty, and you may pay your current tax rate.

One interesting feature of a 401(k) is that many plans allow you to take a loan against the outstanding balance.

I see a 401(k) plan as part of everyone's investment portfolio and I encourage anyone that can afford to do so to invest the full amount they can up to their employer's match. It's like doubling your money.

Individual Retirement Accounts (IRAs)

These are investment accounts that give you tax advantages. They are like a 401(k) that you can open even if your employer doesn't offer a retirement plan.

Like 401(k)s they come with contribution limit restrictions, can offer a variety of investment options inside them, etc.

IRAs can come in both Traditional and Roth structures. They also come in other, such as Self-employment accounts (SEPs). The most common IRA I help folks with are Rollover IRAs, where a person has changed jobs and they roll their old employer's 401(k) into an IRA. This gives you more control over the account and keeps you from having scattered accounts.

If you can afford it, I recommend having a fully maxed out 401(k) plus contributing to an IRA each year.

Real Estate Investment Trusts (REITs)

I enjoy investing in real estate and have in the past. However, there are times in my life where I wanted real estate in my investment portfolio without having to actively own real estate. The best way to do that is through REITS.

If you understand the concept of mutual funds, where you can invest in a multitude of publicly-traded stocks and other investment categories through our pool of investment, then just **think of REITs as a mutual fund strictly for real estate investments**.

In a REIT you are buying shares in all of the properties that the REIT owns. The REIT is actively managed by a fund manager. They collect rents, perform maintenance, etc. and then pay you a dividend (**by law REITs must distribute at least 90% of their taxable income**). Plus, you get to take advantage of any growth in the REIT's share price, just like a stock.

REITs invest in all kinds of real estate. There are funds that focus on everyday homes, while some focus on commercial properties such as retail centers and even medical offices.

One challenge with REITs is that they are susceptible to interest rate increases, because they use leverage, i.e. loans to buy properties. In times of high interest rates, REITs don't perform as well, although you still get to take advantage of the dividends they pay out.

Cryptocurrency

If you've been living under a rock and don't know what cryptocurrencies are, I'll give you a brief explanation. Actually, I've asked Gemini to explain it, in simple terms.

"Imagine a digital money that's like sending a text message, but instead of "Hi," you're sending value. This money isn't controlled by any bank or government. It's like a secret code that only you and the receiver can understand.

Here's the gist:

- **Digital:** It only exists online.
- **Secure:** Uses strong cryptography, like a super-secret code, to keep it safe from hackers.
- **Decentralized:** No single person or bank controls it, it's spread out like the internet.
- **Global:** You can send it anywhere in the world quickly and cheaply.

Think of it like a digital ledger that everyone can see, but no one can tamper with. Every transaction is recorded on this ledger, making it transparent and secure.

That's cryptocurrency in a nutshell!"

Not bad, Gemini. Tip - be nice to the AI-bots, so that when they reach self-awareness you aren't included in their Skynet/Terminator hit list.

If that explanation isn't enough, Google is your friend. I'd look for an explanation on YouTube.

Now, here's my personal take and experience with cryptocurrencies.

In their earlier forms, cryptocurrencies were seen as illegitimate currency and believed to largely be used for elicit monetary transactions for things such as drugs, etc. Today, they are more widely accepted and are even available inside funds. The most common is Bitcoin, but there are upwards of over 13,000 independent coins.

Today, CCs (I'm getting tired of typing out the full word) are used in settling monetary transactions between people. But, early on they were largely a speculative investment that people traded. Because of their potential for volatility, I still consider them volatile. But, **I personally believe that they will continue to grow in popularity. So, I am currently holding a few of the more prominent CCs as an investment,** because I believe they will go up in value.

My thesis is pretty simple. If you think about money today, it's largely already digital. When you see your checking account balance at the bank, it's not like that amount of cash is just sitting around somewhere. The number on that screen is merely a digital representation of the money the back owes you. The power of CCs is that all transactions settle on a public ledger where everyone can see that a transaction occurred, albeit with some redacted details for privacy protection. All of the interest and adoption around CCs, including government adoption, signals to me that at the very least, CCs are here to stay. Now, which CC wins out in the long run is harder to guess.

All of that is to say that it is possible to invest in CCs and earn a nice return. I originally bought into Bitcoin when it was valued in the $30k range and sold it when it hit the $50k range. I've made similar trades with Ethereal and Solana.

As a reminder, I covered a few platforms where you can trade CCs in this section.

Please be careful with CC trading. If you don't understand why I'm cautioning you, just go look at the price of Bitcoin over the last five years. It has swung wildly. Sure, stocks can do the same thing. The difference, in my mind, is that there is more historical precedence with stock trading and how to analyze opportunities.

Wrapping up

I've just pumped over 27,000 words of information out from my brain into yours. I hope you have found this information helpful. I realize there is a lot to digest. So, in case you are feeling overwhelmed, here is one last piece of advice.

Work through your financial position in the following order.

Step 1: Build up your cash flow - even when I've had well-paying jobs, I still looked for ways to increase our income. For the past 10+ years I've built businesses on the side and that has helped us get to where we are today with **stress free finances**.

Step 2: Build up an emergency fund - get this to at least 3 to 6 months of expenses.

Step 3: Work on eliminating debt - particularly high-rate credit cards and car loans.

Step 4: Get insured - no one likes thinking about life insurance, but I've seen first hand what happens when a family loses the breadwinner and they don't have insurance. Yes, it's going to feel like a wasted expense each month. Do it anyway.

Step 5: Build wealth - once the above boxes are checked, start investing. Stay diversified. Don't invest with emotion. Automate the process so you don't skip it each month.

Step 6: Protect your wealth - if you have made it this far, work with a qualified tax attorney or Accountant to figure out how to minimize your tax burden, legally 😊.

Stress Free Finances

There is one more thing I wanted to mention. This tip alone will help you live a stress free financial life.

Get a will and health directive in place. While there are free resources out there, I recommend spending a little bit of money, usually less than $1,000, to have this done by a qualified professional. Your family will thank you for it.

Again, I hope you've enjoyed this information. If there is anything I can do to help you, just reach out to me at jonathan@jonathanmillspatrick.com.

Sincerely,

Jonathan M. Patrick

Resources

Here you can find all of the resources and templates that I have linked to in the chapters above. I've done my best to keep them in order, but I can't make you any promises.

Freelance Success Formula email course - free; this 7-day email course teaches you my steps for creating a freelance business.

https://jonathanmillspatrick.com/freelance-success-formula/

The Budget & Retirement Planning spreadsheet - $1/Free; Gum road wouldn't let me host it for free. Plus, lots of unscrupulous people will download my free content and then sell it online for money. But, *you can use the code SFFBOOK at checkout to get it for FREE.*

https://jonathanmillspatrick.gumroad.com/l/financialplan

Credit Card Calculator from TheBalance.com - free; be sure to follow their instructions to copy the spreadsheet.

https://docs.google.com/spreadsheets/d/10eivpy3fqHGSGBZsdWaerWf-B1KeX4lR7iBqBLpJiJo/htmlview

Auto Loan Calculator - free; you can look up auto rates at just about any website for a local bank or credit union.

https://www.calculator.net/auto-loan-calculator.html

Mortgage Loan Calculator - free; this is my favorite tool for estimating mortgage payments, because it includes all of the relevant expenses.

https://www.mortgagecalculator.org/

Stress Free Finances

Schwab's Debt Elimination Calculator - free; the snowball debt elimination method is a simple strategy for paying off debt. When a balance is paid off, add the amount of its monthly payment to the payment for your next debt. Continue doing this until you have snowballed through all your balances and your debt is paid in full. This calculator shows you just how snowballing works.

https://www.schwabmoneywise.com/resource-center/insights/snowball-debt-elimination-calculator

Dave Ramsey's Debt Snowball Calculator - free; this version follows along with Dave Ramsey's Baby Steps process.

https://www.ramseysolutions.com/debt/debt-calculator

Federal Student Loan Aid requirements and link to FAFSA application - free; these are the requirements you have to meet to be eligible, not guaranteed, federal student loan access. On this page there is also a link to the FAFSA application form.

https://studentaid.gov/help-center/answers/article/am-i-eligible-for-federal-student-aid

FREOPP's article on college degree ROIs - free; this article was published on Medium and includes a database of over 30,000 reviews of college degrees and the return on that degree.

https://freopp.org/we-calculated-return-on-investment-for-30-000-bachelors-degrees-find-yours-1f2f3c5e6dac

Transamerica's Risk Tolerance Quiz - free; the article has some good information. But, if you want to skip to the quiz you'll find the link about the middle of the way down the page.

Stress Free Finances

https://www.transamerica.com/knowledge-place/understanding-your-risk-tolerance

Schwab - Schwab.com is the website for Charles Schwab, a well-known financial services company. It offers a wide range of services to help individuals and institutions invest and manage their finances

Robin hood - Robin hood is a financial services company that aims to make investing accessible to everyone. It's known for its easy-to-use app and commission-free trading, which disrupted the brokerage industry when it launched

Coin base - Coin base is a popular platform for buying, selling, and storing cryptocurrencies. It's one of the largest and most well-known cryptocurrency exchanges in the world, particularly in the United States.

Federal Reserve Economic Data (FRED) website - The Federal Reserve Economic Data (FRED) website is a comprehensive, with over 825,000 data series, and widely-respected resource for economic data. It's maintained by the Federal Reserve Bank of St. Louis and provides access to a vast collection of economic data from various sources.

TreasuryDirect.gov - TreasuryDirect.gov is the official website of the U.S. Department of the Treasury's Bureau of the Fiscal Service. It's your one-stop shop for buying and managing U.S. Treasury securities directly from the government online. Think of it as your personal portal to investing in America.

www.ingramcontent.com/pod-product-compliance
Lightning Source LLC
Chambersburg PA
CBHW050307230526
45471CB00005B/2059